BUDDHISM

A Comprehensive Survey of the Early Buddhist Worldview

(A Simple Guide to Understanding Buddhist Teachings and Practicing)

Joseph Nicholson

Published by Harry Barnes

Joseph Nicholson

All Rights Reserved

Buddhism: A Comprehensive Survey of the Early Buddhist Worldview (A Simple Guide to Understanding Buddhist Teachings and Practicing)

ISBN 978-1-77485-157-9

All rights reserved. No part of this guide may be reproduced in any form without permission in writing from the publisher except in the case of brief quotations embodied in critical articles or reviews.

Legal & Disclaimer

The information contained in this book is not designed to replace or take the place of any form of medicine or professional medical advice. The information in this book has been provided for educational and entertainment purposes only.

The information contained in this book has been compiled from sources deemed reliable, and it is accurate to the best of the Author's knowledge; however, the Author cannot guarantee its accuracy and validity and cannot be held liable for any errors or omissions. Changes are periodically made to this book. You must consult your doctor or get professional medical advice before using any of the suggested remedies, techniques, or information in this book.

Upon using the information contained in this book, you agree to hold harmless the Author from and against any damages, costs, and expenses, including any legal fees potentially resulting from the application of any of the information provided by this guide. This disclaimer applies to any damages or injury caused by the use and application, whether directly or indirectly, of any advice or information presented, whether for breach of contract, tort, negligence, personal injury, criminal intent, or under any other cause of action.

You agree to accept all risks of using the information presented inside this book. You need to consult a professional medical practitioner in order to ensure you are both able and healthy enough to participate in this program.

Table of Contents

INTRODUCTION 1

CHAPTER 1: HISTORY AND ORIGINS OF BUDDHISM 4

CHAPTER 2: TEACHINGS OF THE BUDDHA 11

CHAPTER 3: BUDDHISM – THE BEGINNING 16

CHAPTER 4: BUDDHISM ADZ RHILODZORHU 25

CHAPTER 5: HISTORY AND EVOLUTION OF BUDDHISM ... 28

CHAPTER 6: BEGINNINGS: BUDDHA 33

CHAPTER 7: THE PRACTICE OF BUDDHISM 39

CHAPTER 8: A SHORT HISTORY OF BUDDHISM 54

CHAPTER 9: PHILOSOPHY IN NUMBERS: THE THREE JEWELS AND THE FOUR NOBLE TRUTHS, INCLUDING THE EIGHT-FOLD PATH 67

CHAPTER 10: WHAT IS BUDDHISM? 74

CHAPTER 11: MAKING THE FOUR NOBLE 76

CHAPTER 12: WHAT IS BUDDHISM? 84

CHAPTER 13: MAHAYANA, THE GREAT VEHICLE 88

CHAPTER 14: FOUR NOBLE TRUTHS 116

CHAPTER 15: DIFFERENT SCHOOLS OF BUDDHISM 128

CHAPTER 16: KARMA 151

CHAPTER 17: WISDOM: THE RIGHT VIEW 155

CHAPTER 18: THE DIFFERENCE BETWEEN BUDDHISM AND OTHER RELIGIONS 159

CHAPTER 19: COMPASSION 162

CHAPTER 20: THE MIDDLE WAY 167

CHAPTER 21: MEDITATION 173

CHAPTER 22: MISCONCEPTIONS ABOUT BUDDHISM 177

Introduction

Buddhism is one of the most popular religions in the world. It is fascinating and complex, and it is quickly spreading across western civilization. What does it really mean to be Buddhist? What are the beliefs and history of this religion? You may be a seeker of truth, a student or simply curious about the history of Buddhism.

Buddhism is a spiritual path that leads to insight into the true nature and purpose of reality. Meditation and other Buddhist practices can help you change your mind to increase awareness, kindness, wisdom. All those who want to follow a path that ultimately leads to Enlightenment or Buddhahood have access to the thousands of years of experience in Buddhism. A fully enlightened person sees all of reality as it is and can live in harmony with this vision. This is the ultimate goal of the Buddhist spirituality, which represents the end of all suffering.

Some people don't see Buddhism as a religion because it doesn't include worshipping a creator God. The fundamental tenets and principles of Buddhist teaching are simple and practical. Nothing is permanent or fixed; actions have consequences; it is possible to change. Buddhism is open to all, regardless of race, gender, nationality or caste. It offers practical ways to help people understand and apply its teachings to transform their lives, and to take full responsibility for their own actions.

Around 350 million Buddhists live in the world, and an increasing number are Westerners. Although they practice many forms of Buddhism, all are known to be non-violent, have no dogma and tolerate differences. They also follow meditation.

Buddhism, a revered ancient practice, is more popular than ever. It is due to the many benefits Buddhism offers to those who apply its teachings in their daily lives. Buddhism brings peace and clarity to the lives and minds of those who practice mindfulness and meditation. These wonderful benefits can also be part of your daily life if you are attentive to its many tenets.

Buddhism is not a religion in its original form. It is a tradition that focuses primarily on spiritual growth. Buddhists seek to understand the true nature and purpose of life. They do not worship deities or gods. Siddhartha Gautama (the first Buddha) founded Buddhism in Northern India in the 6th century BC. He attained enlightenment in the 6th Century BC and was given the title Lord Buddha (one who has awakened).

Chapter 1: History and Origins of Buddhism

Buddhism is one the most popular spiritual traditions in Asia. It offers a flexible approach that can be adapted to different cultures and still retain its spiritual purpose. Its open-minded philosophy, belief structure and popularity have made Buddhism a hugely popular religion.

Buddha Siddhartha Gautama founded Buddhism. Siddhartha Gautama, a prince who was born in Northern India's Lumbini (now Nepal) in 624 BC, lived during a period of severe philosophical turmoil when the Vedic religion held power and control over the region. Siddhartha Gautama, who rejected Vedic teachings, founded a sect (Sramanas) of ascetics who later became known as Sangha.

Siddhartha Gautama, a young Siddhartha Gautama, lived in the royal palace during his youth. He left the royal palace at twenty-nine to follow his spiritual calling. He stayed in the forest for six years and was able to attain enlightenment at Bodhi Tree, Bodh Gaya (India). His followers were taught the first wheel of Dharma by him, which included the Sutra of Four Noble Truths. The Sutra, also known as the Lesser Vehicle of Buddhism, is the main source of the Hinayanam (or Lesser Vehicle) of Buddhism. Siddhartha taught the second and the third Wheels of the Dharma later, the Perfection of Wisdom Sutras as well as Discriminating the Intention Sutras. These teachings are the source of the Great Vehicle, or Mahayana, of Buddhism.

The Hinayana teachings by Buddha provide detailed information about how one can achieve freedom from suffering, while the Mahayana teachings describe how to lead everyone to enlightenment. These traditions were first developed in India and then spread to other countries. Many people adopted the teachings of Buddha soon after they traveled West.

Siddhartha Gautama taught around 84,000 lessons. His intention was to liberate everyone from suffering.

His teachings became a spiritual movement that became the foundation for Buddhism after his death in 1980. Historians believe that Buddhism began humblely. Some scholars believe it was a minor tradition that Buddha started during his lifetime, based on limited inscriptions and archaeological evidence.

In the 3rd Century BC, Ashoka, a Mauryan Indian emperor, made Buddhism the state religion in India. The political and social environment were favorable, and the Buddhist faith flourished when missionaries spread Buddha's ideas and teachings. Inscriptions on rocks and pillars in Asoka's realm show his support for Buddhist principles. Buddhism was spread throughout the South of India and Sri Lanka during Asoka's reign. This allowed the creation of Theravada, the earliest form of Buddhism. It is also known as the "School of Elder". The Mahayana, also known as "Great Vehicle," was introduced later. The Mahayana supporters believed it could lead more people to the truth than Theravada. They called Theravada Hinayana, which is "The Little Vehicle," an insult and dismissed Theravada.

The Buddha is seen in Theravada as a historical figure that guides people to Nirvana by his example. Worship is most closely related to the veneration and worship of historical Buddha's relics. A temple's fundamental features often include a tooth or a hair. Mahayana considers the historical Gautama to be the last in a long lineage of Buddhas. According to legend, a Buddha exists in the spiritual beyond and is available to help others. Bodhisattvas can also be found there. They can assist mortals and humans who show devotion. Mahayana, unlike Theravada has many semi-divine forms. This allows for both traditional and superstitious worship styles.

Research has shown that Buddhism was the first religion to spread from its origin country to the rest of the globe. It traveled along two routes to do this. Theravada Buddhism spread southeast to East Asia (Cambodia and Burma, Thailand, Laos, and Thailand) during the 1st Century AD. The Kushan Dynasty ruled northern India and Afghanistan in the second century. Mahayana Buddhism was then spread to Afghanistan and northern India. Kanishka, the king, was a champion of Buddhism and explained how it could be beneficial to individual lives. His kingdom was situated along the Silk Road, which is the main connection between China and Europe. Kanishka's support and strategic location were crucial in the spread of Buddhism. Later on, centers of Buddhism, such as Yun-kang, helped spread Buddhist teachings to other parts of China as well as Korea and Japan.

Buddhism spread to Japan, Korea, and China. Korea was the first to print a Sutra on one sheet of paper in 750AD. In 768AD Japan started to distribute printed copies of the Sutras to pilgrims. Wang Jie, a

Chinese printmaker, ordered a block printer in 868AD to make the first Buddhist book. It measured one foot in height and was sixteen feet in length. It was made with sheets of paper that were glued together at their edges. It is the oldest dated printed book and shows a crowned Buddha with his followers. The 9th century saw the discovery of Buddhist silk scrolls, banners, and they became a key theme in Chinese art.

Buddhism spread and new sects developed. In the 6th century, an Indian monk brought Zen Buddhism to China. It was introduced to Korea in 7th century, and Japan in 12th century. Amida (or Amitabha), sects were also founded in Japan between 12th and 13th century.

People who had traveled to the East brought Buddhist texts to Europe in the 18th Century. The translations of these texts into European languages started in the middle of the 20th century. Around the same time, Buddhism began to spread to America as Japanese and Chinese immigrants settled on Hawaii and the Pacific Coast. There are many Western Buddhists living in America, but there are cultural and ethnic differences between them. The temple serves a social, cultural and religious function for Eastern Buddhists in America. Western Buddhists, however, are focused on meditation.

Buddhism is a worldwide religion that exists in many forms. It is the largest religion in East Asia with over 200 million followers. Theravada Buddhism, one of the most popular schools of Buddhism, is found in Sri Lanka and Thailand. The other largest school of Buddhism, Mahayana Buddhism is still being practiced in China and Mongolia. However, its number of followers has declined due to Communism.

Chapter 2: Teachings of the Buddha

First, we need to have a solid understanding of the Buddha's teachings. This will allow us to know exactly what we should do when we set out to live in the world and try to implement the teachings of the revered one. Let's start by understanding the fundamental tenets and principles of the Buddha's teachings.

Dukkha

According to the Buddha, Life is Dukkha or suffering. However, this does not mean there is no pleasure in this world. Dukkha is the true meaning of Life. It means that life is not satisfying by nature. It is also impermanent, but we continue to behave as though all is well and we won't die. The Buddha said that all things in the universe, including ourselves, and even our thoughts, are in constant flux. It is important to realize that the real goal is not to cling to the temporary pleasures we crave all the time.

The Dharma

In essence, the Dharma is the teachings of Buddha. It is the truth that he understood long ago after he reached enlightenment. This truth was revealed to the world for the first time at Sarnath. It is truly the Universal Truth that binds all of us.

The Four Noble Truths

According to the First Noble Truth, death, old age and illness are just a few of the sufferings that humans experience in their lifetime. There are many other types of suffering. He also confirmed the ancient Vedic theory that humans go through multiple incarnations, and that their Karma determines what kind of life they will have.

According to the Second Noble Truth, suffering is closely related to desire. This happens between the processes of birth and death. There are many desires, including not getting sick or ageing. However, there are also desires for power and material objects. Many of these are not realized in this life, leading to disillusionmentment and unhappiness.

The Third Noble Truth, or the Third Noble Truth, is that suffering can actually be avoided by completely abandoning all desires.

According to The Fourth Noble Truth, the key to the absolution of all desires, as described in the third noble way above, is in following the noble eightfold pathway.

The Noble Eightfold Path

Right Understanding. Understanding the world as it is, not what we wish it to be.

Right Intent. To be determined and passionate about the Noble Eightfold Path.

Right speech. Right speech. To speak with kindness and respect to others and to not indulge in gossip or spreading rumors. We all know how hurtful it is to hear harsh words from others. However, we also see ourselves on the other end of the coin when we speak in haste and misunderstand what we mean. We also know how happy we feel when people say nice things to us. This makes us more aware of the importance and importance of correct speech in our daily lives.

Right Action. Right Action. This also means that we must not lie, steal, or kill others, and we must avoid sexual misconduct and the use of drugs and other intoxicants.

Right Livelihood. Respect for all life. A liquor shop would be a bad idea as it would sell harmful products to people even though they might not drink alcohol. A poultry shop would be a terrible idea because it would require the brutal and unnecessary slaughter of chickens.

Right effort. You should put in just the right amount of effort into your daily life. To be able to take positive action, we must have a positive outlook and welcome good thoughts.

Right Mindfulness. Mindfulness is about being present in the moment and fully immersed in it. It is the foundation of mindfulness meditation. This means to be completely engaged in what you do, whether it is sport or cleaning your house. This will help us face our fears and see how they can become so crippling. We will also be able to identify the bad habits we have and learn how to break them.

Right Concentration. This is a way to focus on one object, such as a candle or flower, and see the real world. You will feel surrounded by peace and serenity once you have done this. This will help us to get away from the daily suffering we face.

As we've seen, Buddhism is a religion which works for the good of all people and encourages them live happier, more fulfilled lives in order to experience the true purpose behind human existence. The ultimate goal is to change one's mind. We have greater control over this process because we can make the changes ourselves and not rely on external factors.

Chapter 3: Buddhism – The Beginning

The Origin of Buddhism

We refer to the Buddha as the Buddha because he was once the child a leader of a small town made up of Shakya people who lived at the Himalayas' foothills. Gautama was the name of the child. There were two possibilities for him to become a great religious teacher or a ruler when he was introduced to the world.

Gautama was raised in the most lavish of liberalities for a young sovereign and he undoubtedly displayed many of the characteristics that would make him a great ruler. Gautama was content to live in comfort and royalty, but he was still troubled deep inside. He saw that there were many people in the castle where he lived who suffered from stress, illness, death, and yearning to be religious greatness. He had never heard of such things in the castle.

He began to doubt the value of his lavish lifestyle as he saw others less fortunate than himself. He found it increasingly silly, as major questions of life and death were not being addressed or cared for at the home he was born. He became a wandering parsimonious after his child was born.

He delved deep into the backwoods to find the great educators who lived and taught. Some of the instructors wanted Gautama to become their 'dharma beneficiary', so he spread their teachings. Gautama was intuitive, highly intelligent, and well-thought. Gautama was never satisfied in any situation and took off on his own in a new direction, pursuit of purpose, and way. He was very close to death, and he knew he wasn't getting anywhere in his life. He met a young woman who felt sorry for him and offered food. He found a tree that was unique and he began to contemplate how he would finish his journey.

Buddha explained that everything, from suffering from pain to envy, is caused by negative perspectives. All our happiness and good fortune comes from positive and serene perspectives. He gave steps for how to overcome our negative personalities. Negative personality traits include envy, outrage and numbness. It is possible to build up our positive personalities by building them up. Positive personality traits include empathy, love and shrewdness. This will help us to understand each other and find peace. These techniques are applicable to anyone, regardless of age or nation. Once we are able to understand them, we can share them with others so that they can also benefit from them.

The religion that we now know as Buddhism has been the driving force behind many human achievements, the source of remarkable social accomplishments, and a lasting and important guide for the wellbeing of many people for over 2,500 years. Every person, regardless of their background, is following the teachings of Buddha today. What are the Teachings of the Buddha?

Who is The Buddha?

Buddhism was founded by the Buddha. The honorary title "Buddha", which means "one who is awakeful" -- the feeling of having reached enlightenment, and is now awake to reality, is called Buddha.

Siddhartha Gautama was the man who would become noticeably Buddha. He was born around 2,600 years ago as a prince of a small region near what is now the Indian-Nepalese border. Although he was raised in a world of great comfort, he could not be satisfied by the material pleasures of his youth. He left his family at 29 to seek out a deeper meaning in the remote forests and heaps of North-East India. He was mentored by the most brilliant religious rationalists and spiritual instructors of his day, but he found it insufficient. At that time, he was fighting alone against the path of self-embarrassment. He took that practice to extremes of self denial but without much success.

He was 35 years old when he sat under the Bodhi Tree's branches in May. This forest was located near the banks of Neranjara and he built his brain in quiet, profound reflection. He used the extraordinary clarity of such a mind with its sharp, penetrative power and conditions of profound inner stillness to focus his awareness on the mysterious implications of brain, universe, and life. He was then able to access the most important Enlightenment encounter, and he became known as the Buddha. His Enlightenment was a profound and inclusive insight into the path of psyche, and all wonders. This Enlightenment wasn't a revelation from a heavenly being. It was a revelation that occurred without the help of anyone else, in the light of the highest level of contemplation as well as the clearest experience of his brain. It meant that He was no longer subject to hostility or hallucination. However, he was freed from all shackles of hostility and hallucination, having completed the consummation and unshakeable peace of all internal enduring.

Buddhists believe that he has achieved a state of being beyond all other conditions. Normal experience is dependent on circumstances -- childhood, brain science sentiments, observations -- but Enlightenment cannot be conditioned. The Buddha is unattached to covetousness and disdain, and portrays opportunity with shrewdness and empathy. Edification is the process of gaining knowledge about the most fundamental workings and causes of life. This allows him to see the reasons for human enduring, the issue that began his journey.

The Buddha lived 45 years and had seen much of northern India. This helped him to understand. His education is known in the

East as the Buddhadharma, or the 'instructing the Enlightened One'.

He reached out to people from different backgrounds, and large numbers of his pupils received Enlightenment. They taught others, and a continuous chain of instructing continued right up to the present.

The Buddha was not a God, and he did not claim to be one. He was a man who, by colossal exertion in heart and mind, freed all confinements. He believed that every being could attain Buddhahood. Buddhists regard him as a perfect person and guide who can guide us all towards Enlightenment.

Buddha believed that the psyche could be in any situation under a condition that was dynamic and that all that arises is a result of causes. Even a state of rest was not everlasting, and all encounters were only temporary. There was no place for self-seeking security or individual permanent quality. When he gave up on this desire, the Buddha was able to enter the unlimited stream of the universe in which he was an inundated participant. "I am not it yet, but it is all of me." State. Each of these seemingly isolated things was seen by the Buddha as co-taking an interested and converging in a brought together process of all inclusive change. One root process of communication was an extraordinary flux. Everything was associated with the beginning of that flux, just as water from a spring is associated back to its source. Transpersonal understanding allowed him to shout metaphorically that he was also there, where the morning star was.

The routine in relation to Buddha entails an examination of brain procedures under test states of contemplation. It's an internal type of research, as opposed to external. Similar to a test, this approach is logical and logical. It is also the focus of modern Science's investigations. From many perspectives, the Buddha could be considered the primary researcher.

These inward effects of inward inquiry are uncannily similar to the results of cosmological investigations by today's physicists, and brain research by clinicians. Despite their completely different approaches and differing expectations, there is no real clash between Buddhism and Science. This parallel may offer some consolation to fledglings. We live in an extraordinary mystery, but here is a religious perspective that is not inconsistent with the deep sciences of our age.

Chapter 4: Buddhism Adz Rhilodzorhu

It might be worthwhile to do some research before we start to do that.

What is idz Buddhism?

Majjhima Nikaua: "Thidz doctrine is idz troubling, difficult to dzee and diffisult in understanding, calm, dzublime not within the dzrhere logis, dzubtle to be understood bu the widze."

Buddhidzm has a slear belief in the afterlife and I believe it is valid. Dictionary.com defines philosophy as "the rational invedztigation and rinsirledz truthdz and rrinsirledz knowledge or being."

Thidz is indeed dzomething which fits into Buddhidzm Veru dznuglu. But to invedztigate themdzelvedz if you find:

"...these are good things; they are not blamable. Thedze thingdz can be rraidzed by the widze. When observed and undertaken, these thingdz will lead to benefit.

Not to mention, the Buddha's teashingdz emrhadzized personal practice and adhering to moral rrinsirledz above anu dogma.Even in regarddz to the Five Presertdz, the Buddha doedzn't describe them as divine laws, but adz rrastisal guidelinedz to follow for one'dz harrinedzdz in this life and the next.Although he mentiondz karmis consequences if one chooses to break them, the Buddha rrovidedz rrastisal benefits to following them aldzo, such adz "freedom from danger...animodzitu...dzudzrision," ets.

Although the Buddha didzsudzdz dzome realitu adzrestdz that people often associate with religion, he also made it clear that the most important aspect of Buddhidzm was how one practices it. This is from the Cula Malunkyovada Sutta where Venerable Malunkyaputta asked the Buddha a series metaphysical questions, such as:

"The sodzmodz are eternal," 'The bodu is finite,' and 'The universe is finite, '? 'The sodzmodz are infinite,'

The Buddha replies to thedze inuiriedz by saying that dzush-uedztiondz don't matter and that asking for dzush is like being dzhot with a roidzonarrow.

The best thing for sourdze is to see a dostor about it.

Chapter 5: History and Evolution of Buddhism

The religion or philosophy of Buddhism has been an inspiration to many civilizations for thousands of years. It has been responsible for many great cultural achievements over the years and has served as a guide to the purpose of human existence for many people all around the globe.

Millions of people, from all walks of life, follow the Buddhist principles today. Many of these people are following the teachings and practices of Buddha to achieve a state that is both mindful and enlightened. This has made their lives happier and more fulfilling. Many people have found that Buddhism has helped them achieve success in both their professional and personal lives. It allows them to let go of negative emotions that have held them back for most of their lives. What are the teachings and concepts of Buddhism? Who was Buddha? Let's find out.

Gautama Buddha (also called "Buddha", or "The Buddha")

Gautama Buddha, a nobleman later to be called "Buddha", was conceived around 2,600 years ago. The exact year is not known. He was a prince from a small area near the India-Nepal border. Gautama was raised in great comfort and enjoyed an aristocratic life. These material comforts did not hide the inconsistencies of life for this curious young man.

Gautama, who was 29 years old, decided to give up all his wealth and inherited fortune to seek the true meaning in life. He moved to the mountains and forests of Northeast India, where he was able to study under some of the most renowned religious philosophers and teachers. Gautama, a prince who was unusually intelligent, quickly absorbed all the knowledge these men had to offer through their teachings. Gautama was unable to find the answers even by the most knowledgeable philosophers. These men were not only brilliant but they could not see the true meaning in life for Gautama. Gautama struggled on his path of self-mortification and took the practice to extremes of asceticism, but Gautama could not discern the true purpose of life.

Gautama then sat under the branches of a tree near the Niranjana River on a May night. Gautama found himself in a deep, tranquil, and luminous meditation. The tree is now called Buddha's Bodhi Tree. Gautama Buddha was able, with the help of the newfound clarity and the extraordinary penetrative power that emanated from an inner stillness, to focus his attention on the truth of life. He was then able to attain supreme enlightenment and became known as Lord Buddha, The Awakened One.

Buddha was able to attain the greatest insight possible into the nature of the mind, and all other phenomena in the world through this advanced state of enlightenment. This enlightenment wasn't given to him by a divine being. It was something he achieved through meditation. Buddha was freed from the grips of delusion, cravings, ill will and ill will at this advanced stage of enlightenment. This meant that Buddha had escaped all the negative emotions and inner suffering that he felt. He had achieved a state unshakeable peace.

Studying and practicing Buddhism can help you discover your true nature or deep-rooted roots. The end result of this path is called "Buddhahood" or "enlightenment". It is possible to incorporate Buddhist practices that emphasize mindfulness and meditation into your life. These practices can help you continuously improve your self-awareness, kindness, awareness, wisdom, and other qualities. Enlightened people can see the reality of reality clearly and live harmoniously according to their profound vision. This state of being, which is Buddhism's ultimate goal, is what is meant to be the end of suffering, and the beginning of a new life free from the stress and anxiety that plague most people's lives.

Chapter 6: Beginnings: Buddha

Gautama Siddhartha (or Siddhartha Gautama as it is written in Western texts) was the man who founded Buddhism. He is also known as Shakyamuni and was born in Nepal more than 2,500 years ago. Gautama was a prince from a noble family and lived in the Himalayan foothills.

Historical accuracy

It is hard to determine how true the history of Buddha is. These stories are very old, and have been told many times over in different languages. Some stories are retold over and over. This chapter will discuss some of the most widely accepted facts about the life of Gautama Buddha.

Although most texts refer to his father's title as a king, and Shakyamuni, as a prince in the texts, historical texts show that their region was a republic, not a monarchy. His father could, therefore, have been a sort of regional leader of the republic, akin to a tribal chief. The Gautama family was, regardless of their titles, a prominent family in the political system.

The Buddha's early years

Legend has it that his mother dreamed of a white Elephant entering her body, before she gave birth to the prince. He was also predicted to be a political leader or a spiritual leader. His father tried to steer him away from the spiritual path in order that he could become a king.

He was well-trained as a soldier and educated. He was a gifted athlete, both intellectually and physically. He married at the age of sixteen. Gautama enjoyed all the luxuries of palace life as a Prince.

According to the legend, his family kept the pains of life from him. He was a slave to pleasure and wealth. Gautama's father was not happy with the decision and the young prince had to leave palace life. Gautama also experienced worldly suffering, what are known as the "four signs" while he was out of the palace.

He saw four signs: an old man (with a sick face), a corpse and a monk. Gautama saw these signs and realized that everything he had in his life was temporary. They could all end at any moment: his health, youth, wealth, and life.

The renunciation

Gautama was deeply disturbed by the suffering of others and wanted to leave the secular world and his position as his father's successor. To end worldly suffering, he gave up his life as a prince to follow his spiritual path.

Gautama had given birth to Rahula at the age of 29. He left his family and palace to lead an ascetic lifestyle and seek answers from teachers who followed the path. He moved from living in a palace and became a wandering homeless man.

He discovered that asceticism wasn't the solution, just like the luxuries of becoming a prince didn't fulfill him spiritually. To find his spiritual answers, he turned to meditation. At thirty-five years old, he reached enlightenment--overcoming the temptations and obscurations of the world, an awakening to the true nature of life. He "became" Buddha at this point. So was born the "middle path", which we now call Buddhism.

Because it offers a way to live between luxury and asceticism, Buddhism is known as the middle path. It's about everyone searching for a way that adds value to the world and minimizes suffering. It means that, despite all the challenges and difficulties we face as humans, we have the ability to overcome them in order to find harmony.

While the middle way is more inclusive than extremes, it does not mean that you should be satisfied with your current status quo. The middle way is about doing what is right for you, while also constantly evaluating your actions to make sure they are helping others rather than hurting them. You don't want to live in poverty. It is not the best thing for you to live in luxury at others' expense.

According to legend, Gautama's renunciation occurred several years later, when Rahula, Rahula's son, was seven years old. His mother took Rahula to the Buddha so that he could ask his father for his inheritance. Rahula's mother wanted to pass the right on to her son because the Buddha wouldn't succeed his father. To the dismay and surprise of his wife, the Buddha instead gave his son a better inheritance and ordained him to the spiritual path. The Buddha was said to have made great efforts to help his son in spiritual learning. Rahula was extremely open to this.

At eighty-eight, the Buddha died. His teachings were carried on by a sangha, or spiritual community.

The term "buddha", which predates Gautama Siddhartha's birth, actually refers to someone who has awoken from ignorance. According to Buddhist tradition, the Buddha is within each one of us. Each of us has the potential to overcome ignorance by kindness, compassion, wisdom.

Meditation and knowledge are the keys to awakening your inner Buddha.

Chapter 7: The Practice Of Buddhism

Buddhism is both optimistic and pessimistic. It is realistic because it has a realistic view on life and the world. It sees things objectively (Yathabhutam). It doesn't falsely convince you to live in a fools paradise. It also does not frighten or antagonize with all sorts of fears and sins. It will tell you what you are and the world around, and show you how to achieve complete freedom, peace, tranquility and happiness.

The middle way

Buddha spoke of the "middle path". The "middle way" was a term used by Buddha to describe the ideal medium between right and wrong.

The Eightfold Path

The Buddha presented the Eightfold Path in his first sermon after the attainment of enlightenment. The Eightfold Path was described by him as the only way to escape all of life's suffering. These teachings must be followed every day if you want to live a happy, healthy, and enlightened existence.

Right Understanding

Bhikkhu Bodhi stated, "The Buddha's tool to free the mind of desire is understanding." Real renunciation does not mean that we have to give up all things that are still dear to us, but rather that we can change our view of them so they no longer hold us back. Understanding the nature of desire is possible when you pay attention to it. This understanding allows us to see things in their true context. It will all be done by itself without any need to struggle.

Wisdom is the key to right understanding. This is not dependent on intellectual ability or the number of years you have lived. The right

Four Noble Truths

Dukkha - The truth about suffering

According to Buddha, "...Birth can be stressful, aging can be stressful, and death can be stressful. Suffering, lamentation, despair, pain, distress, and sorrow are all stressful. Associating with the unloved can cause stress, separation from loved ones is stressful, and not getting what you want is stressful. The five clinging-aggregates, in short, are stressful.

"Dukkha" literally means "life is difficult" or "life's suffering". Although it sounds pessimistic, this truth is essential. This is the feeling of suffering that we have when we are unable to feel whole or attached to the temporary.

Samudaya: The Truth about the Cause of Suffering

Buddha stated, "And this, the noble truth, the origination stress: The craving that makes further becoming -- accompanied with passion & delight now here & now -- i.e. the craving for sensual pleasures, craving to become, craving non-becoming."

Samudaya is the truth. Our suffering is caused by greed and attachment. We desire what we don't have, and we want it for all eternity. But once we have it, we feel empty. This keeps us stuck in a cycle of looking for the next thing that will make us whole. Worse, we attach to everything temporary. We want to keep everything we have, whether it's money, material, or people.

The Truth about the End of Suffering: Nirhodha

Buddha stated, "And this truth is the noble truth about the cessation stress: The remainderless fading, cessation and renunciation. relinquishment. release. letting go of that very desire."

To end your suffering, you have to get out of the "nirhodha" cycle. Although it's not an easy task, it's possible. It is important to learn to let go of the urge to grab for more and to accept that nothing is permanent.

The Truth about the Path That Frees Us From Suffering -Magga

Only the truth of "magga", is the way to end all suffering. The Eightfold Path is the only way to truly live in Dharma.

Right intention

The Right Intention refers to our thoughts. Our actions are important, but so is our thoughts.

Giving to charity to help others, for example, is a good idea. But giving charity to make others feel better is not.

Buddha spoke of this in the Dhammapada. "All that we are" is the result our thoughts. Happiness follows a man who acts or speaks with pure thoughts. It is like a shadow that never leaves him.

Right speech

Bhikkhu Bodhi wrote that truthful speech is, in the sphere interpersonal communication, a parallel with wisdom in the private understanding.

The Right Speech doesn't mean being truthful or saying what is factual. It's about using your gift of speech to help others.

This means you cannot say anything that could cause harm to another person. This does not mean you must lie or be kind. It just means your words can't be used to harm or deceive (example: gossip, impolite language, slander, etc. You can.

Listening to what is being said to us is a must. As we receive attention and ideas, we must also exchange our attention. This is essential to maintain harmony and balance.

Right Action

Bhikkhu Bodhi said, "Beings own their actions and enlightenment. They help their followers maintain clarity and guide them on a path to compassion and mindfulness." They are the heirs to their actions. They are born from their actions and are bound to them. They will be heirs to whatever good and bad deeds they perform.

We must make good choices each day in order to follow the Eightfold Path. Buddhism does not have a set of rules.

Instead, it has a series of personal commitments or "precepts", which outline the correct actions. These precepts were the way the Buddha lived his life.

Five Principles

Refrain from Living the Life of a Living Being

Buddha stated, "One cannot be called noble if one harms living beings." One is noble if he or she does not harm living beings.

Life is precious and should be preserved. This applies to both direct action and negligence. It is just as bad as if you step on an ant, or spray it with poison. We must instead observe and understand the ant so that we can respect its life.

Refrain from Taking Things Not Given

Although this precept is commonly misunderstood to mean "do not steal", it covers much more. This precept does not only apply to stealing from someone's home or reaching into their wallet, but it also applies to taking other things (e.g., their time, energy or resources).

This is an example: going to the grocery shop. Imagine you are outside looking for a parking spot. You can find a spot right next to your door, but you also have a spot at the back of the lot. The closer spot is taken despite your physical ability to walk. This is an example where you take what isn't yours. Although you had the chance to offer that parking spot to someone else, you chose to do it yourself.

Let's suppose that after parking your car, you decide to go in and buy bread. The storm is approaching and the whole grocery store is almost out of stock. There are only two loaves remaining when you reach the bread aisle. You decide to take two loaves instead of one. This is stealing something that isn't yours. This is not theft. You aren't paying for the bread, but you are taking it from someone who might be in need.

This precept focuses mainly on generosity, and the Perfection of giving. Giving in any way is the Way of Buddha. It could be charity, or corrections for past mistakes. The best way to keep balance is to give with no attachment and to receive without gain.

Recall my examples. Instead of parking in the front, park in back, and walk. Don't expect anything in return. Giving for the sake is giving, and you'll be free from greed and selfishness.

Monk Shohaku Okumura said, "When you understand this teaching in that way, it simply creates another standard to measure winning and losing."

Avoid sensual misconduct

This precept was once used to prohibit monks and nuns from engaging in any sexual activity. They weren't allowed to marry and had no children. Depending on their sect, some monasteries allow monks to have children and wives.

This precept is highly controversial for lay Buddhists. It is believed that it prohibits premarital sexual activity, although not all sects agree. All sects agree that sexual misconduct refers to any kind of predatory, exploitative, or harmful sexual act.

Avoid False Talk

This precept is all about honesty. This precept is not about telling lies or half-truths. It's about using your gift of speech positively. It is about being helpful and beneficial to others. False speech is when your intention is to deceive others, by hurting them or making yourself look better. Even if the words were true, it is false speech to say that you are speaking with the intention of benefiting yourself.

Let's say, for example, that you are looking for a promotion and your coworker Sarah wants the same job. Sarah arrives late at work one day, and you tell your boss. Although your words are true, your intention is to make Sarah look better and get promoted. However, it's important to keep your intentions clear. It is not a way to gain anything, but you must tell the truth.

Avoid using intoxicants

Intoxicant does not just refer to drugs and alcohol. It is anything that can distract from the pain in this world. It could be television, music, phones, or food that can distract us from seeing the world through a clear lens. These things can lead to addiction, which can reduce your desire for wholesome fulfillment. The misuse of intoxicants can make you more dependent on this world, which can lead to further suffering.

You don't have to avoid all of these things. The Middle Way suggests that you learn how to find the right balance between misuse and use. It is important to know your limits. You must be open with yourself to determine if you are being distracted from your path to enlightenment.

Right Livelihood

The Right Life is about pursuing a career that is in line with the Way of Buddha. You should not compromise your beliefs just to have a job in this temporary world. You might think of a dangerous job as a mercenary or butcher, which is true. There are other professions that might be less obvious.

You cannot work in a store that employs exploitative labor. Telemarketers often lie to or scam customers, so you can't work in them. Because you may be asked to defend someone who has caused damage or to prosecute someone who did nothing wrong, you cannot be a lawyer.

Although it may sound overwhelming and confusing, this only asks one question: Am I hurting anyone? If you are able to look at your career and say you aren't, then you have the right job. However, if you have doubts, it is worth considering a career change.

Right effort

It is all about making the effort to do the right thing. To live a healthy life, we must put in hard work and be disciplined. You must put in effort to change negative habits, strengthen the positive ones, create new healthy behaviors, and prevent ignorance, anxiety, envy, hatred, or greed.

Let's take the example of painting your home. Your walls used to be white, but they have yellowed over time from neglect. It is not enough to just paint the walls over and forget about them. It is important to understand the reasons why your walls were damaged in the first place. You need to accept the consequences and learn new ways to maintain white walls. You can simply paint over yellow paint and it will fade.

If you put in the effort, you can make a difference in your life. But if your mind isn't open to the possibility, it will be difficult to change your life.

Right Mindfulness

Being present and aware in every moment is the essence of Right Mindfulness. It is about being aware of our surroundings and our relationship with the universe.

There are four frames to Mindfulness

Mindfulness for the body

Mindfulness of your feelings

Mindfulness in mental processes

Mindfulness is a state of mind that cultivates mental qualities

Being objective is key to Right Mindfulness. It's about observing the world with an open mind and not letting your opinions cloud your judgement. Bhikkhu Bodhi said that Mindfulness "brings to light experience in it's pure immediacy." It exposes the object as it was before it has been covered with conceptual paint and overlaid with interpretations.

Right Concentration

Bhikkhu Bodhi said, "Like an unmoved lake, the concentrated mind acts as a faithful reflector, resolving to see everything exactly as it is."

Focus and ability to focus on one thing is the key to Right Concentration. This can be achieved by meditation or chanting. You will be able to experience the Four Absorptions (or dhyanas) if you succeed in your practice. This will enable you to harness your concentration with clarity.

These pages can be referred to often to help you remember the Four Noble Truths as well as the Eightfold Path. Knowledge is the key to unlocking your path to enlightenment.

Chapter 8: A Short History of Buddhism

Buddhism

It is the only religion in which Buddhists don't worship any gods. They follow the teachings Buddha Shakyamuni, who is the ancient man who has been enlightened. People do not worship this man in Buddhism. Only his teachings are respected.

The belief in this religion is that problems and sufferings can be attributed to a negative mind or a confused mind. Happiness is also derived from positivity and a peaceful mindset. Buddhism says that it is important to develop the ability to comprehend clearly. To be truly a friend to all human beings, it is important to cultivate love and kindness.

The primary practice of Buddhism is to take refuge. This means that you depend on the Buddha, Dharma and Sangha. The teachings of Buddha are Dharma, while Sangha is the Buddhist community of monks or nuns.

It is not a religion for many people. Many people believe that God is their creator. However, Buddhist do not do so. They instead follow the teachings of an educated man.

The Founder of Buddhism

A man who had reached enlightenment was the founder of Buddhism. He was also known as Buddha. His Clan name was Gotama or Gautama. His original name was Siddhartha.

Siddhartha was born at Lumbini in the 6th-4th centuries BCE. He is located near Kapilavastu and Shakya republic. He died in Kusinara (Malla republic), Magadha Kingdom.

Although he was born to a Royal family, he quickly renounced his position as a prince. Many people know him by his many nicknames, including:

Shakyamuni

Siddhartha Gautama

Sage of Sakyas

Gautama Buddha

Gotama Buddha

Siddhartha

Sakyamuni

Meaning of Buddhism and Buddha

Buddhism is derived from the word "budhi", which means "to wake up". Buddhism, then, is the philosophy of awakening. Is Buddhism a philosophy? Two words are what give rise to the word theory. "Philo" means love, and "sophia" means wisdom. It basically means love of wisdom. This is also the meaning of Buddhism. It is more than a philosophy, it is a supreme philosophy.

The teachings of Buddha are known as Buddhism in English. Buddha refers to those who achieve Bodhi. Bodhi means wisdom. The literal meaning of Buddha means awakened and enlightened. Buddhism is basically the teachings and wisdom of an enlightened individual.

Birthplace of Buddha

Lumbini can be found in Rupandehi, Nepal. It is a Buddhist pilgrimage spot. According to Buddhist tradition this is where Queen Mayadevi gave birth in 563 BCE to Siddhartha Gautama. He became Buddha after receiving enlightenment.

Lumbini was then located between Devahada, Kapilavastu and Devahada. These two places are located in Nepal.

It is also stated in Sutta Nipata (a Buddhist script verse number). 683 Buddha was born in Lumbineyya Japada's village Sakyans.

When did Buddhism Originate

Buddhism was founded in the late 6th century B.C.E. Buddha Shakayamuni, a former prince, began living in a forest and renounced his position as a ruler. He found enlightenment while living in the woods under a Bodhi Tree. He then began to teach the path of enlightenment to others.

Where did Buddhism originate?

Buddhism was born in North-Eastern India. It was born in an ancient kingdom. This kingdom was called the Kingdom of Magadha and is located in northeastern India's west-central Bihar state.

The Life History of Buddha

Life Before Enlightenment

Birth

He was a Royal Prince. "Shakya" is the name of the royal family where he was born, while "Muni" means "Able One". His mother was Queen Mayadevi, while his father Shuddhodana.

Dream of the Queen

Queen dreamed one night that a white elephant, which had descended from heaven, entered her womb. That night,

Queen conceive a child that was powerful and pure.

Instead of feeling pain after giving birth, she saw a vision in which she held a branch of a tree from her right hand, while gods Indra and Brahma took the child away painlessly.

The Delight of the King

The king was overwhelmed by the feeling of fulfillment when he saw the baby for the first time.

The Young Prince

The prince was extraordinary. He was an expert in maths and all sciences. He was fluent in 64 languages. He did all this without the need for an instructor. He once told his father that he could count every atom in the universe in half the time it took to draw one breath. Although he didn't need to go to school, he did so as his father requested. He was proficient in martial arts and archery. He was a great communicator of spiritual meaning, and he would encourage others to follow the spiritual path.

Witnessing Suffering

Prince would sometimes visit the capital of his father's Kingdom to see how the people lived. There, he met seniors and patients. One time he saw a corpse. These experiences made him realize that all people must experience death, sickness, age, and birth. He realized that only fully enlightened Buddhas have the ability to help people. So he left the palace, and Buddha then went to a forest to practice profound meditation until he attains his enlightenment.

Marriage of the Prince

To stop Prince from leaving the palace, Shakya's family asked the king for a marriage. They hoped that the world would change Prince's mind. His resolve to leave the palace was not affected, but he married to make his father happy. He served as a prince in the palace and devoted his energy to Shakya's people every way he could.

Ask by Prince

He was 29 years old when he saw all the Buddhas from 10 directions come to him and speak in unison. He had previously resolved to become Conqueror Buddha in order to free all living beings from the cycle of suffering. It is now time to do it.

Prince told his father that if he could grant him permanent freedom from suffering, birth, life, and death, he could stay in the kingdom. Otherwise, he would have to leave.

Escape from Prince

King attempted to make the prince stay in the palace, but he changed his mind. He used women, musicians, and dancers to get around guards. He used his magic powers to set the guards to sleep and then escaped the kingdom with the aid of an aide. He made it to the forest, and he said goodbye to his aide. He cut his hair and threw it at the sky, where 33 gods reside.

One of the gods caught his hair and offered him the saffron robes a religious mendicant. He gave his royal clothes in exchange. He became a monk by coordinating his royal clothes.

Attaining Enlightenment

Siddhartha continued his meditation practice until the morning when he achieved varja-like concentration. He was able to remove the final veil of ignorance from his mind by achieving concentration.

Life after Enlightenment

Seven Weeks After Enlightenment

He felt the joy of freedom as he sat beneath the Bodhi tree. He felt calm, free from all thoughts and was blissful and peaceful.

The Buddha sat and meditated on the Bodhi tree to express gratitude for Buddha's shelter during his struggle.

Buddha realized that the devas in heaven weren't sure if Buddha had achieved enlightenment. Buddha built a golden bridge suspended in the air to prove his point. He walked up and down it every day for one week.

Buddha created a beautiful, jeweled chamber where he meditated. Six colored rays of light were released from his body, purifying his mind and body.

Three of the most charming girls visited him during his fifth week and danced in a very charming way. He continued to meditate and they soon tired of him.

The Buddha meditated at a foot of the mucalinda tree. It began to pour heavily. To keep him warm, a huge cobra appeared and wrapped his body in a coil. The rain stopped and the snake became a young man. The Buddha said, "Happy are those who are content." The truth is the only way to happiness. People who are happy have goodwill in the world for all sentient beings, who don't have attachments and have transcended their sense-desires. The highest happiness is to forget the word "I"

Under the rajayatana trees, the Buddha meditated. Two merchants visited the Buddha on 50th day, seven weeks after he had been fasting. They offered rice cakes and honey to break the fast.

His Early Sermons

Buddha visited five monks that had abandoned him months before. The monks did not pay him any respect when they saw him. They all gave up when he approached them, but they failed to maintain their resolve. Buddha gently asked him to not address him, as he had now become Buddha. He invited them to sit down in front of him, and he delivered his first sermon.

Conversion and expansion of an order

He converted more people. He traveled to Rajagriha. The king showed him respect and converted him and his family members. In a bamboo grove, he also built a monastery to Buddha and his followers.

Travel to Kapilavasthu

He met his family and father there, performed a miracle for them and made them believe he was a Buddha. They should not treat him as a family member. He converted his son, father, and wife to the new faith.

Donations from the Wealthy

His teachings were admired by many wealthy people who offered to donate their money.

Opposition to Buddha

There were many obstacles in the life of Buddha. His cousin was jealous and tried to make Buddha suffer. His father-in law also insulted him.

The Final Years

He told Ananda about his imminent death at the Capala shrine.

He then went to Paya, where he lay in a mango tree owned by Cunda, a lay dispile. Cunda invited him to his home. After eating at home, he became extremely ill and it was clear that his last hours were here. He left this world and entered Nirvana that night, just outside of the town.

Chapter 9: Philosophy in Numbers: The Three Jewels and The Four Noble Truths, including The Eight-Fold Path

Buddhism, like any other religion, has many philosophical perspectives. Let's take a look at each one. You can read at your own pace. Take time to reflect and pause as you read.

The Three Jewels

Buddha

The Buddha is a fundamental concept in Buddhism. The "enlightened one" is the Buddha. Buddhist teachings tell of the life of Prince Siddhartha Gatama, an ordinary man who lived approximately 2,500 years ago. Gautama discovered that even after studying the teachings of his tutors, he was still unable to heal his suffering. This was his goal and he decided to pursue his own spiritual path. He found his inner light shortly after sitting under a Bodhi tree,

North India. He had lost all of his negative traits, and was able to see the positive qualities in himself and the world. He was now fully enlightened.

While the Buddha represents an omniscient, enlightened being, it is important to avoid confusing him with the Christian/Judeo/Islamic "God." The Buddha is not credited with creating the universe, nor is he all-powerful. Also, he is said to be an active force that helps people rather than a passive one.

The Dharma

The dharma is the teachings of Buddha. These teachings are meant to help people who follow them, thereby reducing suffering. The dharma asks you to approach the practice with wisdom and not logic. It requires that you trust the teachings and the meanings of the words, and not the teacher. This means that you must let go of all preconceived notions and free your mind.

Buddha-dharma is a complicated theory that can be difficult to understand. The most important thing is to approach your personal practice with steadfast resolution and continue on your journey towards spiritual understanding without allowing outside influences to influence your beliefs. For following the dharma, objectivity, intelligence, enthusiasm are crucial.

After you have decided to start your Buddhist journey, you will be able to choose from a number of scriptures that will help you. These are the traditional teachings and practices of Buddha. The Pali Canon contains the most recent version of traditional Buddha's teachings. The canon includes the Vinaya (the spoken words of Buddha and his disciples), the Sutras and the Abhidharma (the interpretations of Buddha's teachings). Buddhism isn't meant to be rigid so there are other canons, such as the Chinese or Tibetan canons.

Your chosen scriptures should be treated with respect. It is important to treat your scriptures as if they were real. Wrap them in a cloth and carry them around. Never place them under another object.

Remember, you should approach the Dharma the same way as the rest of Buddhism: with patience and commitment.

The Sangha

Different interpretations of "Sangha" are used by Buddhists. Some believe the term encompasses all Buddhists, while others believe it only refers to the entire group ordained monks or nuns. According to the strictest definition, Sangha is only for those who have attained ultimate wisdom.

Buddhism attaches great importance to the idea of Sangha. The monks and nuns of Buddhism are innovative beings who strive to make a difference in the lives of others and help them on their path to ending suffering. They can free themselves from all responsibilities and obligations by making it their goal to help others through the practice Buddhist.

Buddhism recommends that practitioners gather frequently, listen to and respect their elders and avoid the temptations of evil desires to cultivate the Sangha.

The Four Noble Truths

The Four Noble Truths are another major doctrine in Buddhism. These are:

It is part of life to suffer

Buddha taught that pain is an inherent part of life and that happiness is only temporary. There are three types, "suffering" being the most common, which refers to emotions associated with distress, fear, or pain. There is also "suffering from change," which refers the negative effects of a constantly changing world and its consequences, such as destruction and decay. The final category is "all-pervasive pain," which refers to the all-pervasive nature of suffering and the fact that even after death, we can't escape from difficult situations.

Suffering and its Causes

According to Buddhist teachings, suffering is caused by our mental state. The root delusions, or elements in our minds that cause suffering, are anger, ignorance, and attachment.

Nirvana means Peace and Can End Suffering

Here's the "bright side", The Four Noble Truths. Despite the cyclical nature and omnipotence of suffering, it is possible to break the cycle. You can achieve this by reaching the state of Nirvana which is beyond all suffering and pain. Nirvana allows individuals to live a trouble-free life and removes all delusions. To reach Nirvana one must adhere to the Noble Truths of the Path. We will be discussing this next.

The Noble Eight-Fold Path

To attain Nirvana one must follow the Eight-fold Noble Path. This encourages us to help others as well as to create wisdom within our own minds. These practices are the only way to overcome suffering. These are the core principles of The Eight-Fold Noble Path.

1. Right Thought: Avoid negative, incorrect thoughts that could harm you and others

2. Correct Speech: Avoid lying, gossip, or verbal negativity

3. Correct Actions

4. Steps 1-3: Ensure a healthy lifestyle

5. Correct Understanding: The ability of developing ultimate wisdom

6. Correct effort: Meditation requires dedication and perseverance.

7. Correct Mindfulness: When you meditate, keep your attention on the present and space. Instead of allowing your mind to wander to the future, past, or other places, it is best to focus on the present.

8. Correct Concentration

Chapter 10: What is Buddhism?

Buddhism is a religion that focuses on spiritual growth and the attainment of profound insight into the true nature of human existence.

A Buddhist seeks Nirvana. This is the state of enlightenment. He follows the path set out by Siddhartha Gautama, who was the first Buddha to achieve Nirvana.

Buddhists don't believe in personal gods. They believe that wisdom, meditation, and morality are the keys to attaining Nirvana.

Apart from the belief that life is infinite and unending, a Buddhist believes that it is infinite and unending. We can also be reborn many times and continue to suffer and experience uncertainty throughout our lives.

Who is the Buddha?

Siddhartha Gautama (the Buddha) was born into a noble family in Nepal. He was more than 2,500 years old.

Siddhartha Gautama is said to have spent many days contemplating under the Bodhi tree, or the tree of awakening. He was able reflect on his life experiences and eventually reached Nirvana, or the state or enlightenment. Siddhartha Gautama, who was now called the Buddha or "awakened", gained freedom from the inexorable pains of suffering as well as reincarnation.

There are many different types of Buddhism.

Chapter 11: Making the Four Noble Truths are a Reality

Buddhists believe there are "Four Noble Truths" to life. The first truth is that all of life is filled with suffering. The second Noble Truth, which follows a linear thought process, is that all suffering can be attributed to our desires, cravings, and wants. The Buddha realized this and came to the third Noble Truth: Our suffering will end when we can control our desires and wants by being present in the moment and not wishing for anything else.

This thought led to the fourth noble truth, which was the solution the Buddha found for all our discontent and burdensome desires. To reach the fourth noble truth, one must follow the "Eight Fold Path". The eightfold path is a prescribed method of walking through the slings, arrows and world. It requires a shift in your perception. When followed correctly, it leads to:

Right Understanding

If you take the time to understand and analyze the world around, you will be able to identify the causes of unnecessary suffering. You can understand the point of view of another person without being biased and find solutions to problems from an objective point of view.

Deep listening, which Buddhist icon Thich Nath Hanh once called "deep listening", allows you to hear another person's perspective without becoming distracted by your own emotions. Being objective in our understanding allows us to understand the motivations and causes of others.

Right Thought

Once you have achieved this, you will need to "Right Thought" in order to eliminate any negative thoughts or actions. This will allow you to be clear-headed when dealing with your daily activities. If you can cultivate the right type of thinking within your mind, you will be able to get rid of any doubts and fears that you may have had. Right thought is about breaking through preconceived ideas and removing harmful ones. It allows you to see the truth and decide how to respond.

Right speech

You must then ensure that your voice is in control and you use the correct speech. The right kind of speech is when you talk to someone. Avoid slanderous words and talk that is not helpful to others. Be sure to project the image you want to portray to others by avoiding slanderous words and uncivil speech.

We might not be careful and communicate things we don't want to. To avoid this, be direct and keep your focus on the main topic of your conversation. Don't go off-topic. Instead, speak slowly, steadily, and with a steady voice. You can create a dialogue that matches your intended message without getting bogged down in side conversations or intrigue.

This directness should be followed by a willingness to use silence when necessary.

A few well-placed pauses in conversation can make a huge difference. For a Buddhist, silence is the interlude that connects the major milestones in our lives. These controlled pauses can be used to organize your thoughts so they don't run together. Words are like food and require time to digest. The whole point of communication can be lost if we don't give our listener time to absorb what we have just said. Use the "Right Speech"

Right Action

Once you have learned how to use the correct kind of speech, it is time to work on the "Right Action." You need to have the right approach to dealing with others and a sense of compassion in all that you do. The right course of action is one that aims to make a difference in the lives of others and recognizes the impact our actions have on other people.

Buddha explained how our actions can impact us. He explained that theft is not only harmful to the victim, but also to themselves. A thief's bad reputation and reputation will be a problem in all future endeavors. The actions of one person can set bad precedents for the next generation and damage a community. To avoid these negative traits in your personality, you must take the right actions.

Right Livelihood

You should have the right actions, but also the "Right Life" This does not mean that you have to be able to get a job with a high salary. We mean the right livelihood in a holistic way. It must be possible to make a living that doesn't negatively impact others. Simply put, earn a decent living. This isn't the best way to make a living. You are stealing from his neighbors and causing pain for others.

Being able to earn a decent living means having the right livelihood. This is an Indian term for "purpose" and it also means being able achieve your "dharma", which is an Indian term. The right livelihood will allow you to harness your natural talents and make positive changes in the world. This is called achieving your dharma. Always look for the right livelihood.

Right effort

You must also cultivate the "Right Effort" to have a successful livelihood. If you put in the effort, you will be able to focus on what is most important and not waste your time on useless activities. You can learn to control your impulses and only use your energy when it is necessary. The right effort can help you align your life with your goals and fulfill your commitments.

Right Concentration

You can have the right mindset to handle your day if you have the right level of concentration. You need to keep your mind calm and focused. If our mind is not properly trained, we can easily fall prey to discord such as jealousies and feelings of ill-will toward certain people or situations. Our mind can think of many things simultaneously if we don't practice disciplined concentration. The right concentration is necessary to stay focused on the important things in life.

Right Mindfulness

Are you in the right mind? Perhaps the better question is: Are you in your right mind? If we don't practice mindfulness, our minds can become overwhelming with doubts, fear, confusion, and unnecessary thoughts. We must practice mindfulness every day or our minds will become cluttered with mental clutter.

The right type of mindfulness will allow you to let go past experiences and assumptions. This will enable you to focus on the present moment and not get distracted by past associations. The theater of the mind is where all our fears, doubts, and anxieties are played. We are the actors of this theater, so let's get rid of them and allow ourselves to focus on the present moment without worrying or worrying. Right Mindfulness should be a part of everything we do.

Chapter 12: What is Buddhism?

Contrary to popular belief Buddhism does not advocate worshipping gods or creators. Buddhism is a religion that encourages spiritual growth and practice, which lead to insight into the true nature of reality. Buddhism is often considered a philosophy rather than a religion by many. Buddhism can help you develop wisdom, awareness, kindness, and a sense of peace. Over thousands of years, the Buddhist tradition has been a valuable resource for all those who want to follow its path.

The Buddhist path leads to Enlightenment. Enlightenment refers to a person who can see the nature of reality clearly without distractions.

Many people don't consider Buddhism a religion. In the Western religions, there is worship and a creator. Buddhism is not like that. Buddhism offers simple teachings that can be applied to any life, regardless of race, gender, sexuality, or nationality. Buddhism is a way of life that accepts all people. You can use the Buddhist teachings to transform your life and take full responsibility for it.

The next 13 chapters will look at the origins of Buddhism, the main teachings, and how to apply them in your daily life to attain happiness and peace on the path to enlightenment.

The Schools of Buddhism

As Buddhism spread throughout Asia, it split into many sects. Although there are differences in the scriptures and rituals, they all follow the same basic teachings of Buddha.

There are two main schools of Buddhism: Mahayana and Theravada. There are sub-schools within these two schools, but there are very few differences between the major schools and the sub-schools.

Theravada: This is the predominant form of Buddhism in Cambodia and Laos, Sri Lankan, Thailand, Burma, and Thailand.

Theravada Buddhism is a school that emphasizes direct insight through critical analysis and personal experience.

Mahayana: This school dominates in China, Tibet and Mongolia, Japan Korea, Taiwan, Nepal, Taiwan, China, and most of Vietnam. It is much more diverse in its sub-schools than the Mahayana school of Buddhism, so blanket statements are harder to make.

Theravada, which is older than the other schools of Buddhism, claims to be closer to the original teachings. It is ultimately up to you to decide which one is closer or further from the original truths. The sectarian divisions after Buddha's death led to the birth of Mahayana and Theravada.

There is a big difference in the way that both major schools of Buddhism view Enlightenment. Theravada emphasizes individual Enlightenment, while Mahayana believes all forms of existence are void of self. This is why they have different views of Anatta, one of the three universal truths.

Theravada has a smaller number of sub-schools than Mahayana. Theravada uses Pali forms instead of the Sanskrit standard terms forms, while Mahayana uses the Sanskrit form. This book will mainly use the Sanskrit forms for words. There are also places where you might find the Pali word.

Chapter 13: Mahayana, The Great Vehicle

Mahayana is the most well-known stream of Buddhist thought among the many. This school of Buddhist philosophy is the most well-known and is also the one that is most popular. Mahayana Buddhism, which means "great vehicle", teaches that anyone can attain complete enlightenment.

The "bodhisattva path" (the fully enlightened being), is also known as the "bodhisattva car". This is because the vehicle carries the practitioner towards enlightenment and serves all people. Enlightenment is more than a personal accomplishment. It is a gift to the whole world and a message of peace for all living creatures. Bodhisattva is to fully engage in the process of transferring the joy and happiness from enlightened being into this world for the spiritual well-being of all people as well as the joyful integrity all that is.

Dharma

Many people are familiar with "dharma", the name of a woman in a popular TV show. It had a humorous effect and reflected the flighty nature that the woman was married to, who wasn't able to live the hippie lifestyle as her parents or his wife. Dharma is a place of joy and laughter. Dharma is a place where wisdom can be found.

Another Sanskrit word, this one has no translation into English. It refers to various thought strands in Eastern religions like Hinduism or Jainsim. The word is used in Buddhism to refer to a system or cosmic order and law. After attaining enlightenment, the bodhisattva becomes a "bearer" and "keeper" for the wisdom gained through spiritual ascension. The bodhisattva has reached the Dharma level and is now ready to share this wisdom with others.

The task of the bodhisattva, who is responsible for regulating the cosmos towards enlightened action, is a huge one. The bodhisattva is the keeper and protector of wisdom. It is his responsibility to defeat the causes of suffering with wisdom. The enlightened lightens the path of the vehicle and shares the joy of Dharma to all who wish to share in the illumination of the way from darkness, attachment, and suffering.

The bodhisattva speaks the truth by speaking "satya", which is the truth. The two words Dharma and truth are identical in intent. Dharma, however, is a greater and more powerful truth because it is a dynamic expression of that truth. This truth is the foundation of our harmonious cosmic reality. This truth is what we all share in, and we can all find it by getting in the car and searching for it. The truth is something that the bodhisattva can't help but share with others.

The teachings of Buddha are the best way to codify the Dharma for Buddhists. They contain the most complete truth. The wisdom of these teachings, as we saw in the last chapter's mantra, is a gateway to cosmic truth. It allows the enlightened to enter the cosmos with all its harmony and our unique, cooperative role in it.

The Five Aggregates (Skandhas).

An aggregate is a group of items. Buddhism teaches that we are nothing more than a collection or experiences. The idea of the self is a core principle in Buddhism. Importantly, Buddhism encourages the rejection of self in order to reach Nirvana. True existence is not "the self". It is only a part of many parts that make up our essence, and all of life around us. As everything around us, we are either an object or a experience. All fall under the guidelines of the Five Aggregates. Buddhism teaches us that each individual is composed of five parts. These are form, sensation, perception and mental formations. Buddhism asserts that people are made up of all these parts, and not an individual entity. These parts change constantly, so the idea of impermanence is a hindrance to our quest for enlightenment. Let's take a look at these parts, also known as The Five Aggregates and Skandhas.

The first aggregate form (Rupa) refers to both the physical body and the material objects surrounding it. This includes all things, including trees and oceans. It is our "material form". It is made up of four elements: earth (solidity), water(cohesion), heat (fire), and wind (motion). Because it corresponds to our physical sense organs, (i.e. Eyes, nose, ears and skin. This experience, as with everything else, does not occur without consciousness.

Next is sensation. The next aggregate is sensation (Vedana). It describes how we feel about the objects around and how they affect us. It doesn't matter if the experience is pleasant, unpleasant, or indifferent. However, these emotions are what we associate with something. Buddhism claims that attachment to sensation can lead to Dukkha. This is one of the Four Noble Truths and the Three Marks for Existence. Sensation is where we suffer. These will be discussed in greater detail later.

Perception is the third. Samjna is perception. It refers to the sum of all thinking. It is our way of conceptualizing and reasoning about experiences. Perception is how we identify our experiences.

The fourth aggregate is made up of two parts, mental formation and volition. Mental Formation and volition are both the aggregate of habits, as well as what influences our reactions to our experiences. Mental Formation can be described as the way our brains remember repetitive exercises. These exercises are no longer relevant to our minds once they have been stored in the body via repetition. Volition, on the other side, determines how we react to our experiences and has moral implications. These consequences can take the form of wholeness or un-wholeness and also have neutral effects.

There is consciousness. Consciousness acts like a blanket that wraps around the four other aggregates. Because consciousness is the only thing that exists, nothing can exist without it. In its simplest form, consciousness refers to awareness. We are not aware of what we experience, and some levels do not experience it.

The Five Aggregates are a group of five entities that work together to help us be aware and make sense out of our experiences. Buddhism says that they are always present, even when we sleep. As you read this, all five aggregates are present in your life. Physical form refers both to what you are looking at and how you feel about the book. The experience of consciousness is when you are aware of what you're doing. Perception identifies the page. Sensation adds an emotion to the experience. Volition gives you a reaction to it (dozing off, engaging in reading or closing the book).

This collection of factors is part of every experience. It is therefore important to have a clear understanding of their meaning. But it is even more important to remember that these factors are not independent and cannot be learned without experience. Because they are dynamic and always changing, the Five Aggregates are called "processes" rather than things.

The Four Noble Truths

Buddhism asserts that the only way to truly understand "self" is through enlightenment. We are now one step closer towards understanding ourselves. We must first understand what is preventing us from achieving our happiness. Buddhism teaches that the world is full of illusions and that this illusion leads to unrequested desire which can lead to unnecessary suffering. The Noble Enlightened truths are a Buddhist philosophy that seeks to alleviate suffering in this way. These are:

Dukkha, the Noble Truth, states that the world cannot fill the hole in us. Unhappiness in this world is inevitable. It is often inevitable to experience sickness, sadness, anxiety, loneliness, and other negative emotions. Even if our environment is perfect, they can still affect us. You could be enjoying your favorite dessert with your partner and still feel unhappy. Real happiness is short-lived. No matter how much happiness we may seem to have, our happiness soon becomes unhappiness. This can be explained simply by how we constantly ask for things and then find it overwhelming and overbearing to receive them. Our reactions to life's perils are the biggest problem. Because things don't always go our ways, we are constantly in suffering. And because of our relentless search for perfection, our efforts to achieve the impossible will cause us to continue to suffer.

Dukkha, the second of the Four Noble Truths, is based upon our insatiable needs and how they lead to attachment. We actively seek out what we consider desirable and enjoyable. Life is a fluid and changing experience. It brings with it events that don't satisfy our constant desire for pleasure. Not only do we live and die often because of our desire for pleasure but also because we cling to it to avoid unpleasant experiences. This is what leads to unhappiness and short-term happiness. Our own negative emotions, such as anger, hatred, or greed, are what cause us to act without thinking.

We strive to make every experience enjoyable and perfect. This driving force is sometimes obvious, such as when we play competitive sports, but most of the times we don't. This steadfast pursuit keeps us from being truly happy. We all know that no one and nothing is perfect. Yet, we keep trying to find the right formula to be happy. We will be disappointed and suffer in the process.

Consider your morning coffee. You go to Starbucks every morning, and you order the exact same cup of coffee each time.

They seem to always get it right. Sometimes they make a mistake. This small error will likely impact your entire day, regardless of whether it was Starbucks making a mistake or someone else doing the coffee. Your day will be different. You will spend most of your day complaining about how the extra-caramel caramel macchiato was not very special. To turn the tables and try again the next day, hoping for a better outcome.

We refuse to accept that there is no perfect person or thing. Instead of being defined by our inability or unwillingness to attain perfection, we must learn how to discredit the notion of perfection.

Dukkha is also referred to as one of Three Marks of Skandhas (Existence). For the sake of understanding why we are not able to find true happiness, it is worth mentioning the other two marks of existence.

Anicca is the second Mark of Existence. It refers to our inevitability. All that we do, achieve and have is temporary. This impermanence is what allows us to escape from our self-existence.

The world and we are constantly changing. No matter how much we try, nothing will ever be the same forever. This is something we know for a fact. It is not that we don't know this, but rather that we refuse to believe in impermanence fully. Instead, we continue to face change with frustrations and opposition. We are still bound by our material possessions and let them dictate our existence, whether they be mental or physical. To achieve peace within ourselves, we must be able to separate ourselves from the imperfect world.

We often picture our first meeting with someone, be it a friend or a lover, in the best possible way. If the first date goes well, we are happy and optimistic about the future. We imagine all the great things that could happen with this person, and we make unrealistic expectations about how the relationship will turn out. We become frustrated and uncertain when we see the person having a bad day.

Because relationships, just like all things in this world, are temporary and should be treated accordingly. While this does not mean that we should avoid having "relationships" with others, it is important to recognize that there are things that cannot be controlled. We can avoid feeling frustrated by the constant flux of life by accepting this view.

A more basic example of our inability deal with impermanence is the way that we handle disasters. Imagine that you live in an area with a lot of trees. There's always the chance of a tree falling on your house and causing damage. It's something you've seen happen and you have insurance in case it does. But, because you live in the same area for your entire life, you aren't sure it will ever happen. It happens, and it's unbelievable.

We are all aware that Buddhism teaches us to be detached. It simply means "Don't let the things get to you." It is more than just not caring. It's a complete understanding of our place in the world, so we can be at peace with each other. It's not that things aren't important; it is understanding that they don't last forever.

Anatta, or the "nonself", is the final and most important of all the Three Marks. Buddhism, as we have discussed, teaches that "self", however familiar, is not a permanent entity. It also teaches that "ego", which is the byproduct of "self," is not an entity. To achieve inner peace, we must let go of our ego. We need to see beyond our individual selves and become more aware of the world around.

Buddhism says that the only thing we must let go of is our "self", or ego. Buddhism says that the ego, or personality, is a delusion. We are not individuals in any sense we think we are. Once we let go this belief, we can attain Nirvana.

Before we move on, I bet that you are asking yourself this question: What is "self?" What does this even mean? It's very simple. The persona that we have created for ourselves is "Self". This is the person we choose every day. You might imagine yourself as someone who is calm and doesn't let things get to you in stressful situations. In an effort to become the person that everyone tells you, you go to great lengths to try to be that person. Buddhism teaches us how to let go the personalities we have created and to recognize that our need to be a "self" defines us as a block to our path to enlightenment.

Buddhism teaches that all suffering stems from the belief that we are independent, permanent beings that exist alone in the world. We cannot understand impermanence. This is why we are unable to adapt well to changes. Because we are unable to see the changing world around us because we believe in our "self". Ego can limit our perspective. We all know the expression "there are two sides" when it comes to a story. This is because storytellers can't see the whole story without focusing on their own "ego". They don't see the story for its metamorphic qualities. According to Buddhism, this is how we view the world. Once we get rid of all confusion about reality, then our problems will disappear and never return.

The fourth and final Noble Truth, Ending Dukkha, leads to freedom from incessant desire and the cycle that causes unhappiness and attachment. We can free ourselves from the death-dealing cycle of attachment and desire by learning to live in equanimity. To do this, we need to replace our ignorance with the opposite. It is better to plan for the long term than seek instant gratification. This is similar to learning a new skill. Although it may take some time before you see the results of your learning, be patient and keep going. It is important to keep our eyes on the bigger picture. We are all connected on a larger scale. The smaller details of our lives should not be overlooked. We must also consider the impact of our actions on the future and the lives to come. We must remember that we all share the same experiences and are interconnected.

The Eightfold Path of Buddhism's Eightfold Path of Buddhism is what liberates you from Dukkha. This refers to the wholeness of the teachings by the Buddha. It includes meditation and mindfulness. These life disciplines help us to be more detached and less prone to illusions. The Eightfold Path to Enlightenment aims to remove "karma", or mental impulses that bind us to certain behavior patterns. Karma is complex and well worth further exploration. Begin your journey to the Eightfold Path to Enlightenment.

Karma

Karma refers to our compulsive tendency to act in a certain way. Karma is defined by Buddhism as something other than "what goes around comes around rhetoric". Karma is the mental impulse that determines how we react to stressful situations. Karma can be described as the inability to eat more than one potato chip. After we have had our first potato chip, our minds urge us to have more until we are able to eat all of them. Did you ever eat all of a food so quickly that you didn't notice it?

According to Buddhism, this is how karma should look. Karma is not just compulsive thoughts and actions, but also affects the body. This is what we see in the example of potato chips: obesity due to eating too many potato chip.

Karma does not have to be bad. The compulsive behavior that karma causes can also explain our sporadic happiness or sadness. Karma can be used to predict our future. Karma is the result of our behavior patterns. We can control what happens to our lives (e.g., the consequences of eating potato chips).

We must also be aware of the karmic impulses that are driven by destructive behavior. This can only be achieved by being mindful. Awareness demands that we are actively engaged in our thinking. This leaves very little room to impulsive behavior. The key to avoiding the negative effects of karma is to take a second to think about our options when faced with stressful situations. Do you remember that little voice in your head we call our conscience? It is there.

You are probably looking for some clarification on the claim that we can predict the future by karma. It is actually quite simple. Because karma is based upon repeated actions, it can be somewhat predicted what we might experience. We can assume that you could develop cancer if you smoke cigarettes. As we all know, smoking can cause cancer. Karmic actions caused your body's reaction to your thoughts. This example shows how important it is to get rid of harmful habits and create new, beneficial ones.

We can reduce our cravings through the discipline of our self towards enlightenment. This will free us from the pain of wanting and attachment to pleasure. We are not able to see life and the world as it really is - unpredictable, mutable and full of many experiences, each having a greater value than the others. This is how we create our own suffering. The Noble Truths are about finding your own balance in the world. This is where you find true human freedom.

The Noble Eightfold Path

Although the Eightfold Path is a departure from Mahayana Buddhism, it can be used to help you find a way forward that can give you a solid foundation for your practice of Buddhism. The Eightfold Path is a useful tool for people who have a structured life and want to fit their square-peg Western thinking into the circular hole of Eastern thinking. Its structure makes it easy for Westerners to feel at ease in pursuing a peaceful and happy life by applying Buddhist philosophy. Friends, let's face it. We're conditioned here to follow a certain schedule and live within certain time frames. This is how we are.

This discipline's structure is compatible with our conditioning, and can be used as a foundation to begin questioning its utility in our lives. It's what we are used to. It doesn't necessarily mean that it's the path to our bliss. In fact, this way of living could be hindering our bliss.

A structured approach to learning how to achieve greater joy and tranquility can prove useful, for good or bad. It is not necessary for you to use it. However, it can help you to see reality differently and find your way forward. Some people may need some structure to let go of attachment, the primacy and desire of the self, in order to make room for enlightenment and personal transformation.

The symbol of Buddhism is similar to the Star of David in Judaism and the cross in Christianity. This is the Dharma Wheel. Each of its eight spokes represents one of eight elements. These elements may be divided into three sections, each representing a factor in "right thinking/action" (orthodoxy/orthopraxy).

These three areas are the "fullness of understanding Dharma", or the whole of Buddha's teachings. Wisdom is the first. Wisdom's role in The Eightfold Path is to find the "right" way to see the world and to be able to discern one's intent in these perceptions. What is your interest in seeing the world differently? Is your outward focus a result of your inner quest for wisdom? Or are you still operating from a delusional view of the world? Wisdom is rooted in the right intention and right thinking.

The second sector is a continuation of the first, and it concerns ethical behavior. Wisdom is the ability to create a worldview that is productively aligned. It is focused on the harmonious functioning of the cosmos by our right intentions. This also helps us to adopt ethical behavior. This includes our choices of words and the knowledge that words can harm or help. Wisdom should guide our actions towards others and towards the whole. It will help us do what is right. Wisdom will guide our thinking and actions, which will lead to more harmony and less suffering. The ethical framework that questions suffering can have an impact on how we live and provide for our families. Are we able to make a living by the suffering of others? Is what we eat contributing to the destruction of the ecosystem or the suffering of animals Vegetarianism can be a hard path for some. Once we understand the wisdom that leads us to less suffering, we can see the chain of suffering that drives our actions when they are not ethical. Vegetarianism is also worthy of consideration.

The Eightfold Path's third and final section focuses on concentration. As we have discussed in this book concentration is the birthplace for wisdom. It is our ability to let go of thinking that causes us to suffer more than others. This allows us to enter the inner palace where the Buddha lives. This fosters compassion. Concentration is a virtue that comes from contemplative and meditative practice. Meditation can help you to improve your concentration. The application of effort (diligence/perseverance) toward maintaining continual mindfulness in our daily living, leads to an existence in which concentration is second nature. Every moment of our lives is a reminder of the ripples that our existence creates in the cosmos. We are able to reach the Eightfold Path when those ripples flow outward from our hearts, regulating the cosmos through our compassion and love. We are one with the inner Buddha.

Here is a detailed breakdown of each condition in the Eightfold Path for those who want to know more.

Right View: This refers to understanding the world as it is through the Four Noble Truths. Wisdom is the right view.

Right Intention: Combines right view and right intention to create the "Wisdom

Path". Right intention can take three forms:

Renunciation is the act of letting go and letting go of attachments to possessions and objects.

Goodwill is about cultivating "loving kindness".

Harmlessness is a result of active compassion for others. We must be willing to take the pain of others

Right Speech: This refers to the compassionate use and expression of speech. It states that we speak honestly and truthfully. There are four components to right speech:

Abstain from deceptive or hateful speech.

Avoid slandering others.

Abstain from abusive or rude language

Avoid gossip and idle talk.

Right Action: Follows the 5 Precepts. (We'll discuss them a bit in chapter 6).

Right living: This is a way to make a living that does not harm others. It is a combination of right speech and right actions that makes up the part of the path that deals with ethical conduct.

Right Effort is the effort to attain wholesome qualities. Right effort can be described as four things:

Preventing the development of unhealthy qualities

Eliminating unwholesome qualities that have been established.

Develop undeveloped, healthy qualities.

You can improve the wholesome qualities you already possess.

Right Mindfulness is being aware of what's happening in our bodies and minds.

Right Concentration: This is achieved by combining right effort with right mindfulness in order to complete the "mental discipline" portion of the path.

We can unite with our inner Buddha to attain a higher level of knowledge and wisdom that is suitable for sharing in the work Dharma as a life-changing personal lifestyle. Your example is your message. This is why you practice not only for your own peace but also for the peace, joy, and happiness of others. This level of development means that you are working in intimate contact with the cosmos to order it with love and compassion, and heal the suffering caused by attachment and desire. This is the final goal of your personal practice - liberation.

You can liberate yourself, but you cannot keep it. Wisdom is yours but it is not yours to keep. These are to be shared through the message of your heart. Liberation will bring you peace and joy that is hard to conceal. You are a link in all of the chain. It is also your oneness. You will be a beacon for others in that unityive bliss. Your joy and freedom will bring others to you and illuminate a path out of the pain of attachment, individualism, delusion, and craving. Your soul has been liberated and you have been commissioned to become a living symbol of the Buddha, who brought the thousands of teachings to the world.

Freedom is a gift that brings about a deep and lasting peace. The answer to the yawning emptyness of our culture and its desperate need for more is equanimity. You already have more. This is enough. You are the terminus of all suffering. It is within all of us to search, find, and share. There is freedom for all in that hope, the hope of a more fully realized humanity, serving Satya in loving recognition, and there is also freedom from the world. All of us may find joy, peace, and, finally, an end the human misery that is so prevalent in this world.

You can be the change you want when the divine within you sees the divine inside others. You are the gospel of peace. As it blossoms both within and outside, the Jewel in the Lotus is visible.

Chapter 14: Four Noble Truths

One is not noble if he or she hurts living creatures. One is noble if one does not harm living beings." - The Buddha

The Buddhas recognize the Four Noble Truths as the true reality and have embraced them.

Buddhist lessons reveal that the Buddha began teaching the Four Noble Truths after he had experienced illumination. These truths show that all beings ache for and hold on to things and states that don't last.

This causes affliction which entraps the creatures within the inexorable cycle of resurrection, endurance, and passing on. However, there is a way out of this vicious cycle. It's through the Fourth Noble Truth:The Middle Path.

The Buddhas encourage those who want to be woken from the cycle to understand and to experience The Middle Path. It is important to understand and practice the Middle Path by first understanding the Four Noble Truths.

Professor Geoffrey Samuels, Emeritus, was a key figure in transmitting the lessons of Buddhism to the West. He clarified that the Four Noble Truths reveal what must be understood to begin the path that leads to illumination.

Here are the Four Noble Truths (Dukkha): Desire or Suffering (Dukkha). The First Noble Truth reveals that it is difficult to achieve one's goals, which can cause torment or enduring.

Many people compare the Four Noble Truths with Indian customary prescription. The First Noble Truth is the analysis. It recognizes the malady and attempts to depict it as Desire or Suffering.

To see how the First Noble Truth can apply to your life, try the following activity. Take a moment to reflect on the last time you felt fulfilled. You may find that the idea of setting and reaching goals often prompts you to have more yearnings. While there are no negative aspects to pursuing your dreams, it is important to not let them stop you from pursuing them.

Samudaya: Thirst and Craving Karma is your thirst for or longing for something, which causes a change in you that will just prompt another yearning.

If you wish to compare the Second Noble Truth with a medical determination, it can be described as the process where you attempt to determine the cause of the infection. Try to recall the time when you experienced agony in the past and then think about what caused it.

Let's say, for example, you feel confused about a trek you have been planning for a long time. Your longing for the outing is what causes your misery. This is a common occurrence. It is because of this that it is considered a fact.

Discontinuance of Desire and Suffering (Niroda). The Third Noble Truth reveals that one can stop consuming or craving food. This will lead to the end to suffering. This is how karma is broken and one is freed from the cycle.

You could compare the Third Noble Truth with the therapeutic similarity concept and decide the cure for the ailment or the anticipation. What does it feel to let go of one's Desire, and thus, Suffering?

It is best to live it. It is often described by the Buddhas as genuine feelings that bring about serenity in this world.

The Fourth Noble Truth: The Middle Path (Magga). The Fourth Noble Truth: The best way to achieve edification, according to the Fourth Noble Truth, is through the routine and wisdom of the Noble Eightfold Path or the Middle Path.

The image of the Middle Path (dharma wheel) is made up of eight spokes, which correspond to each component. The Fourth Noble Truth, which is the section where the doctor recommends the best treatment for your infection, will be helpful if you are unable to contrast it with the medicinal determination.

Ordinarily, Buddhist teachers divide the Noble Eightfold Path into three central divisions: Wisdom (or Moral Prudence), Meditation (or Meditation). Here is a comprehensive list of how each part of the Noble Eightfold Path fits in to every classification.

Additionally, you will gain a deeper understanding of each one: Wisdom. Wisdom is the primary division of the Noble Eightfold Path. It is comprised of the first two: The Right View and The Right Resolve. These two concepts can be understood and honed to achieve the shrewdness necessary for edification.

Right View. The Right View refers to how you should see karma, resurrection. It also includes how you should esteem the Four Noble Truths at top of your priority list, body and words. It acts as a catalyst for resurrection and influences all stages of a person's life.

The Right View helps you to see clearly through tangled thoughts and misguided assumptions. Once you have a clear understanding of the truths, you will have the Right View. American Buddhist educator Gil Fronsdal explained that Right View can be compared with an idea in Cognitive Psychology.

Right View refers to the way your brain views the world and how it influences one's thoughts and actions. Right Resolve Other, also known as "Right Intention" and "Right Thought", is where the Buddhist finds his resolve to refuse to live in a mundane world to embark on an otherworldly adventure.

Moral Virtue is the second division. It is composed of the third through fifth folds: Right speech, Right conduct, and Right life. Most Buddhist teachers consider Moral Virtue to have the training and legitimacy that will lead to karmic and pensive, social and mental congruency.

These are essential to be able to participate in the final division, Meditation. Right Speech The majority of Buddhist lessons describe Right Speech as the restriction of lying, divisive discourse and sit prattle.

To swear off lying means to not talk about anything but reality and to hold on to reality to keep it solid and true. To avoid divisive discourse means to speak only words that contribute to the general harmony of the situation. To avoid harsh discourse, it is to use only respectful, friendly words that are pleasing to other creatures.

It is important to avoid sitting and talking in a monotone. According to the Buddha, Right Speech means that you speak only what is true and valuable, depending on the circumstances and the place. It is best to say nothing at all. Right Conduct, also known as "Right Action", is similar to Right Speech.

It is not just words but also physical activity. According to Buddhist teachings, Right Conduct means the restriction of killing, taking, or sexually unfortunate behavior. To avoid murder, one must refrain from hurting or taking without end the lives of any living being, human or animal.

To be without taking means to refrain from taking anything that isn't offered or given to you in a conscious way. This includes all forms of taking, such as those that are coercive, stealthily, and through misleading.

To be free from sexual offense means to not have to sexually interact with anyone who is not married, of family, guardians, or kin. Right Life expectancy The Right Life expectancy is when you can maintain your goodness while avoiding being the cause of affliction for conscious creatures.

Many Buddhist lessons teach that there is no requirement to exchange individuals, animals, or creatures for butchering, nor should one be required to exchange toxic substances, weapons, or people.

Meditation

Samadhi is another word for reflection. It is the last division in the Noble Eightfold Path. The whole idea is about molding one's mind with the specific goal of gaining insight into the Three Marks of Existence, letting go of unhelpful states, and achieving Enlightenment.

The Noble Eightfold Path's last three pillars - Right Effort and Right Mindfulness - can be achieved only if you are fully educated and dedicated to rehearsing them.

Right Effort Buddhist lessons describe Right Effort to be your quality of mind and will as you achieve great things every day. It's the ability to control your thoughts, feelings, and actions, even when it's difficult.

According to most Buddhist teachers, it takes more Right Effort and malevolence to abstain from erotic desires and/or malevolence. Malevolence includes outrage, disdain and scorn toward any other being. Erotic wishes are improper yearnings that are experienced through the five detects.

Right Mindfulness

This is the part of the Noble Eightfold Path that allows you to become distinctly aware and mindful of the moment. You are aware of your body and you acknowledge it as it is.

This is true for feelings and thoughts. You can become more aware of these states and be able to recognize them. This will allow you to let go of all common cravings and any affliction that may accompany them. Right Samadhi, or the condition of serious concentration) This is the last step in the Noble Eightfold Path. Right Samadhi focuses on removing yourself from all yearnings associated with faculties and unwholesome states.

You will then enter the primary level of focus, the primary jhana. This level allows you to keep connected and support thinking, which will allow you to feel blissful separations.

You will find "unity in psyche" as you move deeper into the second level. You no longer need to keep connected or maintain thought. Instead, this level allows you to experience pure joy from the state of fixation. This unadulterated joy, like every other express, inevitably fades.

The third level of fixation is where you become completely aware and in control over your resources. After you have let go of longing, enduring, and after feelings such as euphoria, or even misery, the fourth level of extraordinary focus is reached.

This level requires unfaltering and immaculate care. Many Buddhist scholars advise that those who want to follow the Noble Eightfold Path should apply all of the divisions simultaneously, and not just one at a time.

Each element is equal in importance and, truthfully, is associated. However, researchers believe that the Last Variable - Right Samadhi- must be reached if the others have been created. How do you feel about the Noble Eightfold Path and the Four Noble Truths now that you've reached the end? Are you averse to their lessons? If you agree with their lessons, then you will be able to grasp the information and apply it in your daily life. If you don't have the ability to do so, you might find the answers in the next section. Particularly, the following section explains the different schools of Buddhism.

Chapter 15: Different Schools Of Buddhism

Buddhism is fundamentally a way to live. The path to enlightenment can be different for each person, as the Buddha said. It has experienced change over time due to both internal and external factors.

It has evolved internally as monks and teachers have developed new methods and systematicized Buddhist practice after studying the scriptures. Externally, Buddhism has changed to adapt to different cultural situations.

While the fundamentals of Buddhism aren't changing over time, there have been subtle changes to their interpretations. There have been Westerners who have tried to learn Buddhism and become ordained Buddhists, while others have focused more on practical applications.

Theravada Buddhism, the earliest recorded Buddhist school, is still in practice in Sri Lankan and Vietnamese. This is the closest form to original Buddhist practice, with a clear separation between laymen and monks. It is composed of reading the original texts, meditation, and the begging tradition of the monks.

Buddhism found a culture with a long lineage of myths and deities when it reached Tibet. Although the Tibetans adopted Buddhism, it was intertwined into their local culture. The Tibetan Buddhists combined the traditional rituals with strict monastic practices. They created a hierarchy for Buddhist education and the order in which monks should be placed.

Lamrim, a textual account of the stages of the path, was first published in the 11th century. These are versions of Atisha's "A lamp to the path for enlightenment" elaboration.

This text divides each person according to how they view this life and what they want to do.

- A less fortunate person should focus on the positive aspects of birth and consider impermanence or death.

- The laws of karma and suffering should be the focus of the middle person. They also need to consider the benefits of liberation from pain and transformation.

- The four Brahmaviras are the boddhisatva vow and the six paramitas. They make up the superior humans.

These texts are meant to help the practitioner follow a logical path on his spiritual journey.

The tantric view of Vajrayana is a Tibetan form. It uses visualization techniques to meditate, which can help one release suffering quicker. This is because humans are susceptible to attachment. It is by focusing on dissolving this attachment that they can achieve enlightenment.

The west's spread of Tibetan Buddhism had implications for the state of Buddhism in Asia. Different Buddhist thought schools are beginning to work together and share ideas and practices.

Tibetan Buddhism taught that revered lamas who preserved the teachings were more important than monks of higher standing in the past. They are now speaking out for a wider audience, including beginners. It is also possible to address gender issues in Buddhism. An order of fully-ordained nuns was born out of western nuns who were fully ordained from other traditions.

The Western science of the mind has greatly benefited from the efforts of the Dalai Lama. This has made progress in Tibet. Translation of written material allows monks from the east to understand the basics of western science.

The west has spread Buddhism to Tibet, which has helped the Tibetan culture break its dogmatic worldview. Buddhism is being kept in its original form.

Buddhism found a simpler way of living when it reached Japan and China. The original religion was reconstructed with the Japanese roots Zen Buddhism.

Two schools of thought have emerged in relation to achieving enlightenment. By introducing Zen Koans, long meditational practices and long meditation, the focus was on dramatically changing the mental state.

The community of Sri Lanka gave patronage to minor Theravada traditions. These traditions were dissolved after the 12th Century.

Some Mahayana practices were also introduced to major Buddhist schools that are still based on Theravada traditions. Mahayana monks were known to recite Mantras and count prayer beads.

India has been subjected to the caste system, and Buddhism by default is an example of their implication. It's no surprise that the Dalit (untouchable), caste, which has distanced themselves from the system, has adopted Buddhism. Dr. B.R. is a political activist from the Dalit caste. Dr. B.R. Ambedkar, a political activist of the Dalit caste, has brought back the idea of democracy to India and merged Buddhist ideas with politics.

He merged Marxist political ideas in his book "The Buddha, his Dharma" and suggested that Buddhism and political activity could bring equality in society. This would result in less suffering, according to his opinion. Although Buddhism is known for its avoidance of social problems, there have been exceptions.

The Vipassana movement's birth is perhaps more significant than the idea of change in Buddhism. The Vipassana Research institute has become the most influential and modern Buddhist organization. Vipassana was also promoted among non-Buddhists. The organization has provided classes to businesses and institutions.

Because Japan's society and culture are technologically-oriented, Buddhism has been subject to scientific research. Japan may not be a popular destination as the outsiders view it.

Implementing Buddhist ethics and practice could be a huge benefit to the Japanese society. The Japanese are known for being overworked. Because the Japanese have become more like people from the west, societal norms can be very rigid. It is possible to introduce Buddhism to science and offer hope that it will be a gateway into a larger audience.

China was under the rule of Emperor Xuanzong when the three Kaiuyan masters arrived. They established an esoteric form of Buddhism in the Daxing Shansi Temple. The court supported translations from Sanskrit into Chinese.

They brought a dynamic, esoteric and magical teaching that combined the spiritual world with the material. It contained a detailed mantra formula, rituals and prayers to help protect people or kingdoms, bring rain in droughts and affect people after death.

Their last miracle was what made them so well-liked by the Emperor. The emperor ordered that the upper classes favor their teachings over Daoism.

They were not popular under the rule of the next Emperor, which resulted in the persecution of Buddhism. However, the teachings survived and were passed on through a secret lineage monks. They even made it to Japan through the Shingon esoteric school.

Four major schools of Buddhism thought emerged from the original teachings and interpretations of Buddha. These are called lineages in Buddhist nomenclature. These teachings can be interpreted and adapted from personal experience, practice, and meditation.

At the moment, there are four Buddhist lineages:

- Theravada

- Mahayana

- Zen

- Vajrayana

Vajrayana can be considered a part or practice of Buddhism (and not a particular lineage) by some Buddhist schools.

Theravada

Theravada, a Buddhist lineage with the most similarities to historical Buddhism, is Theravada. It is written in Pali Canon, an ancient form of Buddhism. It is a form of Buddhism that originated in Sri Lanka, but has since spread to other parts of Southeast Asia. It is also the lineage most Buddhist emigrants follow.

Theravada's characteristics are knowledge first, followed closely by practice and ceasing to suffer. It had strict rules for monks, which led to the internal divisions that were experienced in the past.

Theravada's attitude towards insight is to expect it to come instantly. This is similar to Vipassana and sounds like Zen Buddhism. The most comprehensive written knowledge of Buddhism is found in Theravada.

It is considered conservative but it is still regarded as the source for modernist Buddhist traditions. The main reason could be that many people who come in contact with Buddhism meet Theravada first, and that the main concepts are very similar to the original teachings.

The second lineage, Mahayana Buddhist, is the most popular. This term comes from Boddhisatvayana, the Buddha who used it as a vehicle to enlightenment.

Mahayana

Mahayana teaches that one cannot attain full enlightenment by following only their own spiritual path. Therefore, benefits should be for all sentient beings. Monks should prioritize sharing their insights, while lay practitioners should meditate to develop a mind that is free from the idea of self.

The Buddha is regarded as a kind of deity in Mahayana. He is composed of three parts. Meditation can be practiced by visualizing Buddha, seeing yourself as Buddha, or repeating the name Buddha.

Mahayana's teachings are made up of many texts that may have different meanings, but all can be true. Mahayana's goal is to attain bodhicitta or Buddha-hood as quickly as possible. This is because enlightened beings are most beneficial to other beings.

Zen

Zen is perhaps the most famous school of Buddhism. It originated in China and has heavy influences from Taoist culture as well as yogic practice. Zen has experienced a surge in popularity in the west. Many western students are attracted to Zen Buddhism. Zen meditation is the most common way to study Zen. Focusing on your breath is a good place to start. The next stage of study is simply sitting. This is called shikantaza. Spiritual awakening occurs when you meditate. Although Zen, like other schools of Buddhism, is based lightly on the Four Noble Truths of

Buddhism and the Eightfold path of Buddhism, it is not a moral teaching. It is not based on any spiritual connections or beliefs. Zen students sit still and do not move, allowing their thoughts to flow freely, and allowing them to merge with the universe.

The study of Zen is a simplified version Buddhism that doesn't refer back to scriptures or doctrines. Zen Buddhism is about finding the meaning of your life. It is not a simplified version of Buddhist doctrine or scripture.

Vajrayana

Vajrayana is the fourth lineage and is often considered part of Mahayana. Madhyamaka and Yoga-Cara are some of the Mahayana derivatives. Buddhist logic is a scientific western analysis of the reasoning Buddha used. It seems transcendental to me and still accurate.

Mahayana practice includes the ability to chant Mantras and be mindful of the Buddha. The Buddha taught the dharma in a way called "Great Vehicle". It is a historical view of the dharma through its evolution over the years. This is true not only for the dharma, but also for its clarity and understanding. However, it must be remembered that it was a continuous process.

Vajrayana can also be called Esoteric Buddhism. They create a system that allows for faster attainment of enlightenment, freedom from suffering, and Tantrayana, Tantrayana and Tantric Buddhism.

Vajrayana is also known by the name "Thunderbolt Vehicle", which refers to a mythical weapon. This symbol is used to describe tantric practices in Vajrayana.

Vajrayanists have accumulated a lot of Tantras that have been used in Buddhist visualization. These were originally used in rituals not conforming to Buddhism, but they were later incorporated and transformed and integrated into Vajrayana.

Vajrayana teaches that the mundane samsara world and sacred nirvana coexist in a continuum. This belief has been held by other Buddhist schools of thought.

Although Vajrayana's insight is often compared with Mahayana Buddhism's, Vajrayana teachers claim that their practice is more effective. Vajrayana's roots are in the teachings of a group of Yogi's who traveled around, so many of its practices and teachings look like a mix of Yoga and Buddhism.

Vajrayana is similar to Mahayana. This path is different and focuses on Buddha-nature. This is to allow the Buddha-nature of humans to be identified with their Buddha nature, and to attain enlightenment.

Vajrayana has a special form of sacred bond between teacher and student. The student goes through transformation. If an outsider hears them, the dialogues can prove to be dangerous. Therefore, they must remain secret from the rest of the world.

Vajrayana's specific practice is to overcome the dual nature. In rituals, impure and defamatory substances from bodily origin can be accepted and used. Sometimes these are offered to the mind as an offering to overcome the dual view.

Tantric practices that involve sex do not aim to provide sensual pleasure, but to help one get closer to Buddhahood, the object of worship. For the sake of nurturing love, emphasis is placed on the female aspects of nature and humans.

What do modern Buddhists do and what should they be doing?

The modern world is full of Buddhist practices that vary between cultures and countries. The Buddhist lineage is the most important factor in countries with a history of Buddhism. This includes the practice and the following of the teachings.

The practice and the following are often inherited in western countries, where there have been many Buddhist emigrants. People of western heritage have adopted Buddhist practices over following lineages. While there are some people who have found a spiritual path to Buddhism and some who have been ordained by the Buddha, most westerners do what is practical.

A third form of Buddhist practice is meditation, which has been developed by traditional Buddhists to be used for therapeutic purposes. This type of meditation can be used for healing, but it can also serve to cultivate qualities that have been developed through regular Buddhist practice and knowledge about the dharma.

It is important to distinguish between modern Buddhism from Buddhist modernism. Although Buddhism has seen many sectarian movements, few of them have any active participants to this day.

The type of practice that is followed by westerners will often differ from the one they are used to. It is easier to fully accept the Buddhist path if there is an active Buddhist group near one's home.

Because Buddhism is a different path than what one was taught and it is difficult to integrate it into daily life, one would need guidance. It would take courage and determination to pursue it alone, as western society and norms can be very different from the ones one seeks refuge in the three jewels.

It is more common for westerners to start the practice because of certain events in their lives. It doesn't matter if it's a mental illness or a physical condition, an agnostic person will find Buddhism more compatible with his natural beliefs than religions which have an omniscient deity at the center of worship.

If one is interested in Buddhism in the west and begins to practice it, it is usually because they are seeking a better way of living or a solution for a problem. A monastery or active Buddhist community can provide guidance.

There are many Buddhist centers around the globe, but Australia is the country with the highest concentration of Buddhism. For advice on how to improve your mindset, there are monks and dharma talks available.

The United States and Europe have made Buddhist practice a part psychology and psychiatric treatment.

Vipassana meditation is the best choice if the patient responds well. Vipassana meditation is well-known for bringing calmness and allowing one to overcome mental difficulties. The therapist must have the necessary skills and understanding to help their patient with Vipassana meditation.

Living in the west can be stressful. Scientists are realizing that medicine cannot treat the root causes of stress. A person who cannot handle reality at its core can only be prescribed so many pills.

A person can practice mindfulness and meditation without having to accept Buddhist beliefs. It isn't necessarily a bad thing, as long as the practitioner has found refuge in these practices, she doesn't have the obligation to develop her spirituality.

The benefits that a western practitioner receives from practicing mindfulness meditation and mindfulness are dependent on her motivation, perseverance, and the knowledge she has. These practitioners are more likely to abandon the five precepts after a certain point because their mental state is not in balance.

It is not uncommon for people who have experienced the benefits of meditation and mindfulness to become more interested in Buddhism and the Dharma. This interest can lead to being more informed or a deeper understanding of the practice.

One aspect of westerners that is difficult to overcome is sexual misconduct and right speech. The first is due to one's attachment to sex while the second is a social norm one has become used to. This is not something to judge or ignore. It is important to approach this from an honest place, with curiosity and love.

It is usually dependent on your upbringing, education, and social status as to how difficult it is to uphold the Buddhist precepts. These precepts are dependent on one's ability to persevere and natural talent. They also require a high level of mindfulness. Language is deeply embedded in our brains. It can be difficult to change speech patterns, especially if one remains among her peers.

It is unfortunate that it can depend on one's status, as being ethical has become a difficult task. It can be difficult to integrate Buddhism into one's everyday life due to one's obligations towards the family or one's own personal material existence.

A Buddhist practice can be a powerful tool to help one self-improvement. If the practice is not based on the core teachings, then it can be a negative tool for the society that the individual is a member of.

If the practitioner is selfish, it can lead to his individual capabilities growing. This is what the Buddhist community calls misuse of skilled means. It is because of this that Buddhist texts are kept as esoteric messages.

Because we have the ability to find information on almost any topic through modern media, Buddhist teachers are more inclined to provide their services to ensure that Buddhist beliefs and practices remain constructive for the public.

There are many therapists and psychiatrists who have worked with people who have mental disorders or have had to deal with them. These professionals often have a deeper appreciation for the philosophy and practices of Buddhism.

Some professionals might decide to visit a monastery to provide better instruction to their patients.

People who have benefited from Buddhism and overcome difficulties such as addiction, depression, or anxiety are often very persevering in their practice. Spiritual progress can be achieved even if you experience difficulty.

People who have not been a part of a family or community but are interested in Buddhism and decide to follow it, often seek out a monastery that allows them to practice their faith in a peaceful environment.

Many westerners have sought work on farms in Sri Lanka to hear Buddhist teachings and concentrate on their practice. They can join a monastery depending on their determination and if they are motivated enough, they might stay there.

One's ideas about Buddhist monastic life may not match reality. Being a Buddhist monk can be difficult. If this was a temporary phase of one's life, then such practitioners will not be able deal with the dynamic of being a Buddhist monk.

Many westerners have been ordained and helped to establish monasteries under the guidance of their teacher. They often give dharma talks that relate to both the mundane aspects of western life and more difficult issues such as illnesses.

Cultural and language barriers can be difficult to overcome. If students don't learn from the original texts or spend enough time learning the skills of being a teacher, the Sangha (community), might offer a compromise between the western lifestyle and original Buddhist teachings.

Chapter 16: Karma

Karma is a term that is used a lot these days. Karma is an idea that holds you accountable for your actions. It is similar to the "give respect, get respected" rule. Buddhism, however, takes a different view on this meaning.

Sanskrit means action. So, Buddhism does not view Karma as an outcome of an action. Instead, it defines Karma simply as the act itself. In Buddhism, Karma is set when you do a willful act. This is called 'fruit'.

According to Buddhist Monk Thanissaro Bhikku Karma is defined as "the act of doing good deeds.""Multiple feedback loops are involved in the shaping of the present moment. Past and present actions influence the future. However, the past also shapes the present."He is referring to the fact that the past is not only reflecting on the present but also the present is reflecting back on itself and the future.

Karma teaches you that your actions can have repercussions and will be noticed. Karma teaches that each step you take has the potential to shape your future.

According to Walpola Rahula (famous scholar),

The theory of karma is not to be confused with the so-called moral justice or reward and punishment. Moral justice or punishment, also known as reward and punishment, is the result of the idea of a supreme being, God. He is thought to be a judge, who gives law and decides what is right and what is wrong. The concept of justice is dangerous and ambiguous. It does more harm than good to the human race. The theory of Karma, the theory of cause, effect, action, and reaction, is a natural law that has nothing to do justice, reward, and punishment.

Karma is taught in Buddhism as well as in many mainstream religions. Islam teaches you to do good for others, in order to expect them to do the same. This is also true for mischief. It is the same thing as Karma. This is a reminder that you can't spread trouble and expect all your desires to come true. It also teaches that anyone who causes trouble for others will be noticed.

Let's take Karma as an example. Imagine your neighbor going through a difficult time. You are aware that they don't have enough food for everyone. You have plenty of food at your home and are able to provide assistance, but you decide not to. Karma is the idea that if you engage in selfish behavior, you will soon find that your neighbor will also adopt this selfish attitude and not receive help.

Karma is the idea that you should do good for others in order to make them good. It's like giving and receiving - the more that you give, you get back. It teaches that you shouldn't be selfish or feel invulnerable. Humility is also associated with Karma. It states clearly that no one is untouchable, and that if someone is trouble, they will be trouble for you. Tit for tat.

Believe in Karma, and live your life accordingly. This means not doing any harm to anyone else. This involves ensuring that every decision we make is right and not selfish. What do we do when we expect the best from doing good? We do good. It's that simple. It can be read in the same way as the "Golden Rule", which you probably already know: "One should treat other people as one would want them to treat me."

Chapter 17: Wisdom: The Right View

The right view is often the first element of the eightfold noble path. This is because most people prefer to begin their journey from the right view, even though it can be started anywhere.

The simplest definition of right view is the correct way to see life. The life we live and the world around us. Only a practitioner can have a correct perception of life if he or she accepts these four noble truths.

In my previous book, I explained how the four noble truths speak about the universality of suffering and how acceptance can free us. This acceptance is the essence right view.

Take, for instance, a situation in which you failed. Let's take for example, you fail an exam. You might be tempted to become angry or feel miserable about the situation. It will help you see the situation from a different perspective. As if you were looking at the situation from a third-person's perspective. You might not only be able pinpoint the causes of this failure, but you will also see that it was inevitable. It's not that you caused it or brought it on yourself. But it is a fact that it was inevitable. That is how you can find peace and understanding in the situation. Momentary peace can be achieved by having the right perspective. The eightfold path's ultimate goal is to bring about peace throughout your life.

This example shows how the right view can be applied to everyday life. It is not limited to outer-worldly responses. Introspection is as important as having a right view. The path of Buddhism cannot be followed if there isn't the right view.

Right view is described by scholars as having the ability to keep your goal in sight.

Your goal in this instance is to attain nirvana as well as inner peace. When you work towards a goal in worldly affairs you must keep it in mind. The Pali Canon gives the example of a trekking expedition.

Your goal, the highest mountain peak in your trek, is right in front of you when you go on a trek. You are focused on the mountain peak every day, no matter what time of day it is.

Similar to the Buddhist path, your ultimate goal should always be your quest for nirvana. Your goal should always be your focus at all times. This is your internal right view.

This refers to being aware and in touch with your inner self, your feelings, and your flaws at all times so you can fix them and stay on the right path.

It is why most people choose to start with the right view. It shelters and helps the other parts. We will discuss right speech under the division precept later in this book. Your goal is possible once you have established a right view. You would have constant supervision over your inner self. This would allow you to monitor what you say and make sure that the right speech is implemented.

Right view means to see the raw, basic nature of everything. Let's take food as an example. It is a driving force for many people.

People love to eat. They even commit atrocities to eat better. They don't have the right view of food. Food is a tool. It is how we nourish our bodies. This is the right view. While food is essential for survival, it is not the ultimate goal of life. If you have the right perspective and can see the true nature of food, you will be able avoid traps such as overeating or lusting for food. This analogy is applicable to almost all things material in life.

The right view allows us to distinguish between the important and the superficial. This distinction will help us to stay on the noble eightfold path.

Chapter 18: The Difference Between Buddhism and Other Religions

We have already discussed some fundamental points that defy the ideologies of others.

No

Buddhists don't believe in Gods, unlike other religions. You can read Chapter 1 to learn more about the reasons why Buddhists don't believe in God.

Nothing lasts forever

They believe everything is constantly changing unlike other religions. They don't believe that a person dies when he eats the fruits of death. Instead, they believe that the human enters the wheel of living.

There is no permanent time

Meditation does not require that one meditate at certain times. This is unlike other religions.

Afterlife

Buddhists don't believe in an afterlife. Buddhists believe that after death, people are reincarnated into another life to pay for the wrongs they did in their previous lives.

Reward or Punishment

Buddhists do not believe that reward or punishment can be granted after death, as opposed to other theists. They do not believe that there is an afterlife. Therefore, it doesn't leave them with the question of reward or punishment in the afterlife. They believe in the laws of karma, which work in this life. They believe that humans pay for their actions in this life, so it is not necessary to have an afterlife.

Paticcasamuppada

Buddhists believe that paticcasamuppada means nothing exists by itself or as a result of coincidences. Everything is interrelated and dependent on each other.

These are the main reasons that Buddhists are different from other religions. It is a book that you should read if you want to fully understand how liberating and open Buddhism can be.

Chapter 19: Compassion

Buddha emphasized enlightenment as a key to Buddhism's foundation. Buddha believed wisdom and compassion were the key to true enlightenment. He believed that these two are like two wings that help fly, and they travel together.

Conventions have very different definitions for compassion and wisdom. They are two distinct things that don't coincide. Wisdom is viewed as something that is purely intellectual, while compassion is interpreted as being purely emotional. This pits them against one another, making it appear that we can't use our full intellect if we are only emotional. We can only assume that wisdom and compassion cannot coexist. This is common thinking.

Buddhism follows a different path. Wisdom in Buddhism is all about consciousness. It's about understanding Buddha's teachings - something completely different to the traditional meaning.

Wisdom and compassion should be practiced together in Buddhism. One is better than the other. Let's move on to compassion. This is covered in more detail. "Karuna" is the Buddhist term for compassion. It can also be translated as sympathy. It's about putting others first and letting go of your personal interests.

It is a very idealistic concept to think of compassion as karuna. It encourages you eliminate all suffering wherever you can see it. It may seem impossible in practice, but it is possible. Buddhism encourages you to keep trying. Buddhism teaches us that everyone can do their best and there will never be more suffering. It's about being compassionate together so the world can be a better place.

You may wonder what compassion has to do with becoming enlightened. Buddhism emphasizes the fact that true enlightenment is in realizing there is no "you" or "me," only "we." By being compassionate and considering other interests, we can open ourselves up to the possibility of selflessness. This is true enlightenment, it says.

His Holiness the Dalai Lama in his book Essence of the Heart Sutra covered compassion in great detail. He wrote:

According to Buddhism, compassion can be described as a desire to help others. It is not passive. It is not empathy. Instead, it is an active effort to alleviate suffering. True compassion requires both wisdom and loving-kindness. This means that one must have both wisdom and loving-kindness.

Integrating compassion in our daily lives means to do good and not expect any return. Although this may sound absurd at first, it is what Buddhism emphasizes: true compassion. To expect a return, even if it's simple appreciation, is to not be able recognize the 'we" part. Are we grateful for water? Do something for each other because we all are one at the end. There are no thank yous or debts. This is called 'Dana Paramita,' which in Buddhism is the perfection and giving. This is because giving results in receiving and both parties require each other. So, how is one superior to another? This is true compassion.

Buddhism teaches compassion, as well as how to teach it. This is where the secret lies: practice. First, you need to examine yourself and confront your demons. We become more open and more aware of what is happening in the world around our lives by letting go of our self-delusions.

The Tibetan Buddhist religion refers to this concept as Tonglen. Pema Chodron, an ordained Buddhist Nun, discusses the topic and claims that Tonglen requires you to first become aware of your own suffering before you can develop compassion for others. Both are interconnected because only by understanding our own suffering can we be able to understand others. Tonglen ignores the conventional wisdom that says suffering should be avoided in favor of pleasure. This allows us to realize the true meaning of selflessness.

Pema Chodron says,

Tonglen is a way to get out of the old trap of seeking pleasure and avoid suffering. It is possible to love ourselves and others, and to also take care of others. It increases our compassion and opens us up to a wider view of reality. It opens us up to the infinite spaciousness Buddhists refer to as'shunyata. The practice allows us to feel the open dimension within our being by connecting with it.

Buddhism insists on the importance of karuna, compassion, without prajna (wisdom), and vice versa. They can only work together towards true enlightenment.

Chapter 20: The Middle Way

Although the term "The Middle Way" is well-known to most people, many misunderstand its meaning. The Middle Way is a way to understand reality at a deeper level that our conditioning minds can handle. Our culture, education, and society have conditioned our minds to see the world in a dualistic way. The mind-body connection is one example of the Middle Way. The mind and the body seem to be distinct from one another. As we can see and feel it, the body is obvious to us. The mind isn't as obvious. The mind is not visible to the naked eye. We cannot touch it. It is therefore understandable to believe that the mind and the body are distinct. This is an example duality. The belief that mind and body are one thing is also plausible. It has been proven that the mind can affect the functioning of the body, and the body can affect the mind.

This paradox is recognized by the Middle Way, which sees the truth in both sides.

Understanding the paradox of separation and unity in all phenomena allows us to avoid traps and make better decisions. Because it is practical, by challenging societal beliefs and looking deeper, we can address the challenges facing society. These challenges are often caused by not understanding the interdependence of all life. Each of the problems we face in the world is caused by our perception of ourselves as separate from all of life. Every action we take has an effect on the rest of the universe. This perceived separation is what causes our suffering, just as with the mind-body argument.

Exercise

You can practice the Middle Way by spending a few minutes each day just looking at the world around. You can become a blank slate for these few minutes. You don't need to worry about your past experiences or your education. Let the world unfold as it is, without imposing any judgments on it. You will see life differently if you are able to view it without any conceptualizations.

Buddha Nature and Enlightenment

The Buddha nature, the purest form of consciousness, is within all beings. It is difficult to express the Buddha nature in words. It is best to imagine the Buddha nature as deep sleep. Pure consciousness is what we can experience in deep sleep. Deep sleep is a state of pure consciousness. We are free from any thoughts. Deep sleep is not a time when we experience thoughts. Because there are no thoughts to describe our experience, we lose any sense of identity and sense of experience. It is possible to feel your Buddha nature, regardless of whether we are deep asleep or awake. Our experience of life will become calmer when we can access our Buddha nature. We are anchored in pure consciousness and the stillness of our silence. We can also enjoy the joys of living. The meaning of enlightenment is to have direct contact with the stillness of Buddha nature while we live our daily lives. According to the Bible, "In this world, but not of it"

Consciousness

Buddhism is ultimately about recognizing that consciousness is the basis of all things. Humanity holds the dominant belief that we are conscious of the world around and that we are physical beings. We also believe we are separate from the world. According to Buddhism, consciousness is the only thing and it is expressed as the mind, functions of the mind and the universe. This is how we see deep sleep. Deep sleep is not an experience because consciousness does not interact with thought. What happens in deep sleep? What happens to you in deep sleep? Deep sleep is something you don't remember. However, you do know you were there when you woke up. This is the most important thing. This awareness is the source of all experience, even those you believe to be yours. This is what the term "oneness" and "unity" refers to.

30 Day Challenge

The Buddhist principles and exercises in this book might seem strange and unintuitive to most people. It will likely take a lot of practice to fully understand the power of these principles. You don't have to do all of the exercises to reap the benefits of Buddhist principles. Simply by doing one of the exercises, you will naturally gain a greater understanding of the others. This 30 Day Challenge will help you get the most out of this book's exercises.

Take a look at all the exercises, and choose those that resonate most with you.

You can make a promise to yourself that each day you will be practicing the exercise or combination of exercises you have chosen. You can only choose one exercise to practice every day for 30 consecutive days. You can do one exercise per day for 30 days if you have selected more than one exercise. If you're really successful, you can do multiple exercises per day for 30 days.

Try to do more practice each day. You can practice meditation for 10 minutes on your first day, but you should try to increase it to 20 minutes each day. You will have more profound breakthroughs if you increase the time that you practice meditation each day.

You may want to continue your 30-day challenge, but this time with new exercises.

Chapter 21: Meditation

You must be in the correct position to meditate. You can also use a wooden chair with a firm base and your feet flat on the ground if you are unable to move. Your back should be straight. You can sit on a cushion, or a stool made specifically for meditation, if you don't have mobility issues. Then, bend your knees. Cross your ankles. Place your hands on your lap, with the strongest hand supporting your other, palms up. Step 7 is actually about meditating and following a consistent pattern of meditation.

Continue to sway until you find the perfect position. You should not skip the swaying movements in the beginning stages of meditation. Otherwise, you might feel uncomfortable halfway through. Grounding is simply a way to ensure that you feel comfortable while in meditation.

Breathing

We've already discussed the proper way to breath. Breathe in through your nose and feel the air moving inside of you. Instead of thinking about it as air, consider it energy. For a second, hold the breath and then exhale. Continue doing this until your breathing rhythm creates the pivot in the upper abdominal. You will be able start your meditation when you are able to maintain a regular rhythm with your breathing. Close your eyes.

Breathe through your nose - For the count of seven, think of nothing other than the breath.

For 5 counts, hold your breath.

Breathe until you reach the eight count.

Count the number 1. This is where you add the number that you are currently on.

While you do this, all you can think about is meditation. It is normal to have thoughts sneak into your head. This is normal if you're not a master at meditation. Recognize the thought, then release it by going back to the exercise above. Continue to breathe this way, and you will use the numbers 2, 3, 4, 5, 6, 7, 8,

9, 10, 12, 14, 15, 16, 18, 19, 20, 24, 25, 26, 27, 28, 30, 32, 34, 36, 38, 40, 41, 52, 58, 59, 61, etc. You will reach number ten when you are done. You will undoubtedly have to return to number one many times. This is normal, and it's what most people do.

The first few sessions should be no more than 35 minutes long. It's better to have shorter sessions that are successful than trying to force yourself into meditation for too long if you're not an experienced practitioner.

You should be focusing on counting and breathing the right way all the time. You should not think about anything else.

Meditation: What can you gain?

Your subconscious can learn to control your thoughts patterns so you can feel at one with it. Your conscious mind is not busy counting or breathing, so your thoughts don't get in the way of you actually reaching within yourself. Meditation can improve your outlook, make you feel more energized, and change the way you think.

After meditation

Respect your body is essential. After a meditation session, your heartbeat and blood pressure will slow down. Don't rush to get back to your daily life. Instead, review your session and make a list of what you could have done better next time. This will help you to learn. This is crucial and will allow you to take a little more time, while your heartbeat returns to normal and blood pressure normalizes. This will allow you to use the thoughts you have to enhance your meditation experience the next time. After you've tried meditation, you can explore other forms of meditation such as mindfulness meditation or chant meditation. However, mastering the basics will allow you to get more comfortable with the discipline.

Chapter 22: Misconceptions about Buddhism

Many myths surround Buddhism. Some are based on rumors that have no basis. There were many misconceptions about Buddhism. Some people studied, but didn't practice, others tried to practice, but received poor guidance. As a result, there was confusion. Modern people don't think religion is important. They believe they only have power and money and nothing more.

Many people believe Buddhism is similar to Christianity, which believes in God. Buddhism doesn't require belief in God. Buddhism teaches you about the purpose of life, which will lead to true happiness. God can save you only if you believe in him and are unable to help yourself. God will give you hope and a path to success. Buddhism, however, believes that each person has the ability to solve their own problems. His followers are encouraged to explore the teachings and be more decisive. They should also take responsibility for their actions and understandings.

Many people mistakenly believe that you are a Buddhist if your robe is worn. However, modern Buddhists are not required to wear robes every single day. Only the Buddhist ministers are allowed to wear them on special occasions, while the members are permitted to wear casual clothing.

Many believe that Buddhists believe luck, and that they bow with their palms together to pray for it.

Although Buddhists believe in luck, they don't pray. If you are able to seek out luck and do not break the Eightfold Path or the Five Precepts, then luck will be yours. They value all life, no matter what it is, and they are open to any future fortunes or misfortunes. A sign of gratitude and thankfulness is to bend and pray.

Buddhism is more popular than other religions and people are beginning to notice. Celebrities from the United States like Angelina Jolie, Brad Pitt, Richard Gere and Brad Pitt have begun to embrace Buddhism.

A misconception about a religion is a judgmental act that will not benefit us. Many misconceptions exist about Buddhism. But the most important thing is that those who practice its teachings live peaceful, enlightened lives.

Conclusion

Because you are ready to seek out more, you have read this book. This means that you are ready to go find your Bodhi tree and sit under its spread branches to learn the lessons from the first manifestation of Buddha nature Siddartha. You don't have to be the first. You are ready to discover a new way to see reality and to find your place within the cosmic order. Eventually that joy will become who you are, which is your truth - your Satya.

Buddhism is not a religion as we think of it in the West. It is a "way". It is a philosophical way to see reality as harmony and joy, rather than threat and misery. It is a way to let go of the culturally-embedded desire for more, more money, and more love - as our desires submerge the sense of proportion and our ability to see the world as it really is. It's not worship of a personal god or the longing to have an afterlife. When there is no desire, there is no emptiness. When there is no desire, there is no suffering. Only joy can be found in finding oneself home once and for all in the infinite compassion of the heart. Only the joy of being a light in a world of illusion is worth it. Christians sing, "This little light of mys, I'm going let it shine." As your peace grows and spills over, yours will shine brightly.

There's more to life than survival. Survival is the level of humanity that is closest to the ground. It is humanity at its most primitive and unaware. We are so much more than this and yet so much less in the end. We can be more in touch with our true nature by releasing ourselves from the egotistical notion that we exist in separate universes. This allows us to be both smaller and more. Both important and insignificant. These designations have very little significance in the vast sweep of cosmic reality. The whole is more than the sum of its parts. It is an operational reality. We all are part of this wholeness. To be free from the illusion of attachment that arises from our desire to have, we only need to recognize it as the truth about our existence.

You will be free to dance in the cosmic whole and enliven it with the light Buddha nature. You will find the enlightenment which brings forth the lotus petals, blessing the whole world with joy and life-affirming beauty.

Be blessed.

www.ingramcontent.com/pod-product-compliance
Lightning Source LLC
Chambersburg PA
CBHW071843080526
44589CB00012B/1095